sew it in minutes

24 Projects to Fit Your Style and Schedule

travels 2006

Chris Malone

©2006 Chris Malone
Published by

kp **krause publications**
An Imprint of F+W Publications

700 East State Street • Iola, WI 54990-0001
715-445-2214 • 888-457-2873

Our toll-free number to place an order or obtain
a free catalog is (800) 258-0929.

Library of Congress Catalog Number: 2005934366

ISBN-13: 978-0-89689-358-0
ISBN: 0-89689-358-8

Edited by Sarah Brown
Designed by Emily Adler

Printed in China

Acknowledgments

It takes a lot of creative and dedicated people to make a book a reality, and I would like to thank all the people at Krause Publications who contributed their talents to "Sew It In Minutes." I especially thank my wonderful editor, Sarah Brown, for all her hard work, brilliant insights and creative eye. My job is easy compared to hers! A special thank you, too, to Julie Stephani, the acquisitions editor who guided me through the first formative steps, and to the gifted photographers, Kris Kandler and Bob Best, who worked so hard to make each and every photograph a work of art.

The backgrounds for the photos are so important, too, and I thank Hansen's Brand Source in Waupaca, Wisc., for allowing us to use their beautiful furniture and accessories as a complement to the projects.

And, as always, I thank my husband Jim, who patiently puts up with it all and gives me his support and encouragement, and my children and grandchildren who make my life so complete!

ntroduction

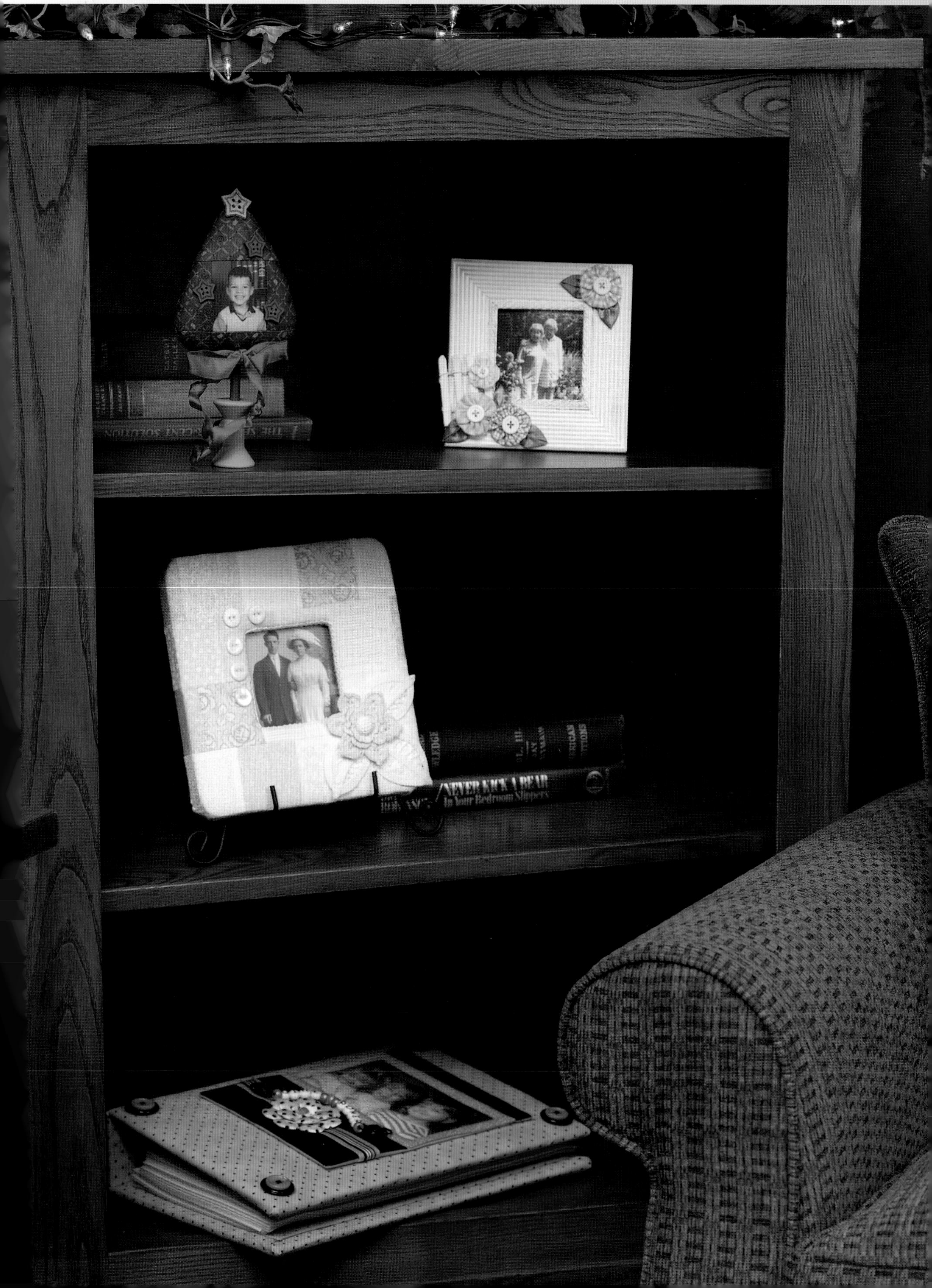

TIME!!! We never have as much time as we would wish for, especially when it comes to crafting and sewing. Our lives are busy and full, yet we need and appreciate lovely things around us, handcrafted with love and styled to our own personalities.

Even if you have only an hour or two to spare, you can still create something truly unique and special. In this book, I have composed six chapters, each with a specific theme — gardening, friendship, relaxing with a good book, a love of photos, sewing and travel — and each chapter has four original projects. Here you will find something to fit your schedule from one hour to an evening. Of course, these time allocations have to be a little flexible, based on how quickly you work and assuming that you have selected your materials and have them close at hand! Each project is based on a completion time of 60 minutes (1 hour), 90 minutes (1½ hours), 120 minutes (2 hours) and 240 minutes (an evening) — so you truly will "sew it in minutes"!

I have also included many little tricks and strategies that I like to use to make an ordinary project extra-ordinary. There are many time-saving techniques and simplifying steps for basic construction that will allow you to focus your creative energies on imaginative embellishments. Also, I share my ideas on ways to transform purchased wares to original designs with a maximum of style and a minimum of time.

So please, take the "time" to read through the chapters on Basic Supplies and Basic Techniques before you begin your own one-of-a-kind creations!

Table of Contents

Basic Supplies

Before you begin any sewing project, it's helpful — and a great time saver — to have all your tools and materials organized and handy. This chapter lists the supplies that I find essential for my sewing designs. Some are particularly useful for those of us with big ideas and little time!

Tools

Using the right tool for the job and keeping that tool in good working order are actually great time savers and make the "creating" process a lot more enjoyable too. This list of basic tools will see you through any of the projects in this book. Need I add that keeping them organized and handy will save time, too?

Sewing Machine

A good basic machine with a smooth straight and reverse stitch and a plain zigzag stitch will work for all the sewing projects in this book. A ¼" foot, also known as a quilter's foot, is very useful for producing accurate seam allowances. Follow the instructions in your machine's manual for routine cleaning and maintenance.

Scissors

You will need a good, sharp pair of scissors for fabric only and another pair that you can use on paper and other materials. A small pair of scissors for snipping threads is useful, too.

Rotary Cutter and Mat

A rotary cutter and mat are not essential tools for these projects, but they are such time savers when you have strips and blocks to cut. They make it possible to accurately measure and cut through several layers at the same time. The 45mm rotary blade is the most common size and if you have the room and the budget, buy a large mat for cutting large strips and pieces and a small mat for trimming.

Rulers

The see-through acrylic rulers are so handy for measuring and cutting with the rotary system. A good, all-around size is the 6" x 24" with ¼" markings and a 45-degree angle line; it will reach across a folded piece of yardage. A smaller ruler, such as a 6" x 12", is easier to use for shorter cuts.

A centering ruler is so handy when adding embellishments for anything that needs to be centered. It has a "zero" mark in the middle and equal marks radiating out. Sometimes I use my "eyeball" for centering, but this ruler really is more reliable!

You will also need a tape measure for some steps such as measuring the circumference of a basket. A good quality tape with easy-to-read markings will last a long time.

Marking Tools

A lead pencil for marking light fabrics, a white pencil for marking dark fabrics and a fade-out pen for transferring patterns are essential tools. For pattern templates, you can purchase template plastic (available in quilting stores) or use discarded plastic lids or lightweight smooth cardboard.

Needles and Pins

Keep an assortment of different size needles for your machine handy and check the package to select the appropriate needle for the fabric you are sewing. Hand sewing needles should include sharps and embroidery needles, sizes 7-10.

Embroidery Hoop

Embroidery hoops keep the fabric taut and make the hand stitching easier and smoother. They are inexpensive, and it's a good idea to keep a variety of sizes on hand.

Iron

Invest in a good steam iron and keep it clean and as close to your sewing machine as possible. The new "mini irons" on the market today are so handy to have plugged in right beside your machine for quick seam pressing and fusing appliqués without having to get up and move to the ironing board.

Good Lighting

A lamp with a bright, cool light will make it so much easier to see true colors, especially at night. Some are available with a magnifier and a clip to hold patterns or instructions.

Fray Preventative

This is one product that I couldn't do without! I use it to prevent fraying on ribbon and trim ends and it can even eliminate the need for hemming on some projects.

Miscellaneous Notions

Look through a sewing catalog and you may find lots of notions that will be useful to you with your specific needs. I just found a seam ripper with a magnifying glass attached!

Plastic Organizers and Bags

Having supplies sorted and stored properly will save so much time and lower your stress level, too. They also help to keep your tools and supplies clean. The best ones are clear so that you can see the contents without removing the lid.

Materials

Fabrics, threads, adhesives and embellishments are at the core of these quick-and-easy sewing projects. If our goal is to attain the most panache for the time invested, then a review of these basic materials is time well spent!

Fabrics

A trip to the fabric store can be both inspiring and overwhelming when you are starting a project. Here are a few guidelines to keep in mind when you are faced with so many choices:

Color: Although I list specific colors in my instructions to recreate the model in the photograph, you may want to substitute colors that complement your home or wardrobe. Bright, bold colors or subdued country shades, pastels or jewel tones, contemporary primaries or Victorian blends — the colors and combinations of colors set a mood and style. I often start with one multicolored print that I really like and then use the colors in that print to select the coordinating fabrics. Often stores and catalogs will bundle together six or eight fat quarters or half-yard cuts that complement each other — a shopping timesaver that makes combining fabrics easy.

Pattern: The pattern of fabrics — geometrics, florals, polka dots, plaids, pictorials, abstracts, stripes and so on — also contributes to the mood and style of your project. Just by using a coordinating variety of prints in various scales, you can really enliven a project even without adding any surface embellishment.

Texture: The physical texture of a fabric — rough, smooth, soft, coarse, sheer — is another factor to consider when making your selections. Besides their effect on the style of the project, some fabrics are more difficult and time consuming to sew and to iron. Good quality, 100-percent cotton fabric is easy to sew, presses well and just generally behaves.

Some of the material lists call for "fat quarters" or "fat eighths" of fabric. These cuts are 18" x 22" and 18" x 11", respectively, and may be found in most fabric stores. Often, these cuts will minimize waste because they are a more useful size. Some projects also require scraps. For all of these projects, a scrap will mean at least 12" square. Please refer to the cutting instructions and/or patterns to see the specific sizes you will need for each fabric.

Threads

Quality is important with sewing threads. Good quality thread is smooth, strong and easy to use. Most of the supply lists call for "matching sewing threads," and by that I mean a cotton or cotton-wrapped polyester thread in a color that closely matches any fabric that will be sewn by hand or machine.

Adhesives

I love to sew, but I'm not a purist! Sometimes the proper adhesive will do the job better and certainly quicker.

Iron-on fusible adhesives have become a real staple for most sewing rooms. Both lightweight and heavyweight versions are sold in precut packages or off the bolt at most fabric stores. The paper-backed adhesive film is heat sensitive and will bond fabrics together, making appliqué so much quicker and easier. They can be used with or without additional hand or machine sewing. Since the brands vary, always follow the specific instructions that come with your fusible adhesive.

Fabric glue is another product that I use frequently for construction and embellishment. The key here is *neatness* — learn to use as little glue as is needed, keep it off your fingers and think twice about where you are putting it before you pick up the bottle! I like a glue with a relatively fast tack (that still has a little time for rearranging), a clear color when set and one that is washable.

Embellishments

This is the fun stuff that truly makes your project unique and personal. Most of us who have sewn and crafted for years already have a big button jar, a box of doodads and drawers of interesting scraps that we can root through when we need something special. But don't despair if you are just starting out, because there has never been such variety and quality to choose from in the stores.

I love buttons — they add color, texture and dimension and come in every color and finish you could want. Vintage buttons, too, have a charm of their own and can often be found at garage sales and secondhand stores. And don't limit yourself to just the buttons you find attractive — the next chapter will show you ways to cover and enhance those not-so-lovely ones, too.

Specialty threads, fibers, ribbons and pre-made trims are so abundant now and the variety is mind boggling. They make a colorful and tactile contribution to a project with a minimal effort.

One of my more recent discoveries is the fabulous selection of possible sewing embellishments sold in scrapbooking stores. Letters and words made of metal, wood and plastic, little mirrors and frames, and adorable miniatures are just some of the possibilities. Begin to look at everything with an eye for how it may be used in innovative ways!

Check out the selection of possible embellishments in the craft store, too. Wood cutouts, beads, charms, sequins, rubber stamps to use with fabric ink, fabric paints, felt and eyelets are all embellishments that add interest to a sewing project. In addition, there are many products available in craft stores ready to be decorated with our sewing skills; baskets, frames and pre-made totes, hats and aprons are all blank canvases awaiting personalization.

There is one more shopping arena I suggest you check out for ready-made embellishments — the hair accessories aisle! You will find wonderful flowers, beaded shapes, ribbons and more in a myriad of colors. They are usually inexpensive and your imagination will find many ways to incorporate these decorative pieces into your sewing projects.

Basic Sewing Supplies

You will need these basic supplies for every chapter:

- Sewing machine
- Iron and ironing board
- Ruler

- Scissors for fabric and paper
- Assortment of sewing needles and pins
- Marking tools and template material

Basic Techniques

Before we start sewing, I would like to detail some of the techniques that I use to make my work quicker, easier and/or more fun! Some are tried-and-true methods that I have pulled from my quilting background and others are simply the result of necessity and invention.

Please take the time to read through this section and become familiar with these basic techniques so you can refer back to them as needed. You will undoubtedly find new ways to incorporate some of these ideas as you design your own home décor and wearables.

Rotary Cutting

There is no doubt that rotary cutting has revolutionized the sewing world and freed up many hours that were spent measuring and cutting. Quilters have embraced the rotary cutter, mat and see-through rulers since they were introduced in the 1980s, but I use mine for simpler projects, too. In fact, I have a separate mat and cutter that I use for felt and batting — two materials that you do not normally use with a rotary system because they dull the blade and the mat cuts do not self-heal as completely with the loose fibers. So when the blade on my quilting cutter gets dull, I put it on my "other" cutter.

1. Smooth the fabric out on the mat and fold it in half lengthwise once or twice to cut several layers at a time.

2. Align the horizontal lines on the ruler with the fold and the appropriate vertical measurement line with the cut edge of the fabric.

3. Cut along the side of the ruler with the rotary blade as you hold the ruler with your other hand. Use firm pressure and always cut away from yourself.

4. Move the ruler and re-align it for each new cut.

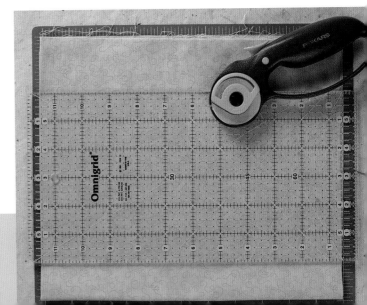

Machine Stitching

Here are a few steps that you can utilize with your machine that will save you time and frustration.

Starting Stitches

When starting a line of stitches, sometimes the threads jam or the fabric gets pulled into the needle hole opening. To eliminate this problem, hold on to the two thread tails as you start to sew or use a small scrap of fabric as a starter. Just start your stitches in the scrap and sew off the scrap and onto your seam without clipping the threads. Cut the starter scrap off when you are finished.

Chain Stitching

Chain stitching conserves both time and thread when you have a number of pieces to sew at the same time with the same color thread. Just as with the starter scrap described above, you will stitch the seams on the first set and then butt the next set of pieces right behind it and continue sewing. When you are all finished, remove the chain of pieces and clip the threads between each set.

Zigzag Gathers

An amazingly easy and timesaving way to gather long pieces of fabric is to use a zigzag machine stitch over a heavy thread. Position the heavy thread along the edge where the gathers are needed and set the machine for a wide zigzag. Sew over the heavy thread, being careful not to pierce it with the needle. To gather, just pull on the heavy thread.

Unless otherwise instructed, the seam allowance for all of the projects in this book is ¼" wide.

Pressing

I think pressing is a very important element in good sewing, but it can distort and damage the fabric if not done properly.

STEAM IRON

Iron a seam in the closed position first to set the stitches in the fabric. Then iron the seam open or to one side as needed. Lift and set the iron and glide it carefully (as opposed to shoving it across the fabric) to avoid any distortion. Use a temperature appropriate for the fabric. If you have a Teflon or fiberglass cover, you will probably want to turn the temperature down since the reflective properties of these covers intensifies the heat.

FINGER PRESSING

You don't have to get up from your chair and walk to the ironing board to use your thumbnails for a quick press — how convenient and it works surprisingly well for small pieces. A hera marker (a scoring tool found in the notions section) works well, too, and can be kept right by your sewing machine.

Fusible Appliqué

Fusible adhesive is a wonderful time-saving product that allows you to appliqué designs to fabric with the touch of an iron. It bonds the fabrics together and eliminates the need to turn under the raw edges of an appliqué. Fusible adhesive comes in two versions: lightweight (easily sewable) and heavier-weight. If you plan to add machine stitching, always use the lightweight. Handstitching can be accomplished with either, but is easier with the lightweight.

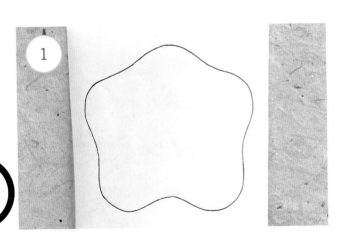

1. Trace the design onto the paper side of the fusible adhesive. Remember that the finished appliqué will be a mirror image of the pattern, so reverse any design that has a definite direction. Letters and numbers must always be traced in reverse. In this book, the patterns for fusible appliqués are already reversed for you.

2. Cut out the traced shapes about ¼" from the pattern lines.

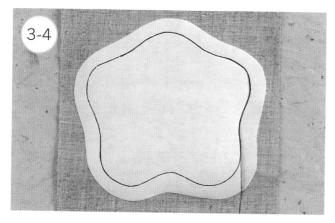

3-4

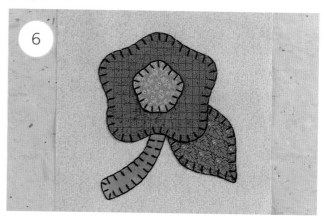

6

3. Fuse each shape to the wrong side of the fabric that you have selected for the appliqué. Each brand of fusible adhesive is a little different, so read and follow the heating instructions that come with the product that you are using. The paper side faces up and the fusible is against the fabric.

4. Cut out the shapes on the pattern lines and remove the paper backing. You will be able to see the film of adhesive on the fabric.

5. Arrange the appliqué piece(s) on the background fabric. The point of a pin or needle is helpful to drag the pieces into place. When you are satisfied with the arrangement, fuse the appliqués in place. *Note:* If you work with your background fabric on the ironing board, you won't have to move the pieces after they are positioned to iron them.

6. Add hand or machine stitching to the appliqués, if desired. For projects that are going to be worn and laundered repeatedly, the edges *should* be secured with stitching. Use a narrow zigzag stitch, a satin stitch or other decorative machine stitches, or hand sew a blanket stitch around the edges.

Hand Stitches

Decorative hand stitching adds dimension and color to your work. You need to be familiar with just a few simple stitches for the projects in this book. Cotton embroidery floss and pearl cotton are the most common threads for these stitches, but try using rayon floss, metallics and even silk ribbons for extra richness and sheen.

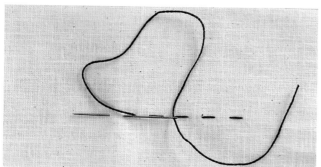

Running Stitch

This stitch is the basic hand sewing stitch and can be used for construction, basting, decoration and, when the stitches are longer and the thread is pulled, for gathering. A hand quilting stitch is a small, even running stitch sewn with quilting thread.

Backstitch

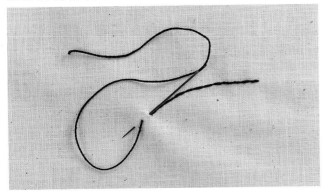

This stitch is useful for embroidering letters and outlines. Use a small stitch to embroider tight curves.

French Knot

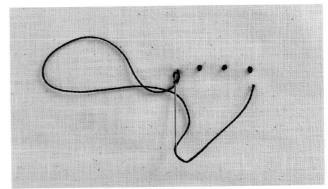

This dimensional stitch is used wherever a dot is needed. The size of the dot depends on the thread used and how many times it is wrapped around the needle, usually twice.

Blanket Stitch

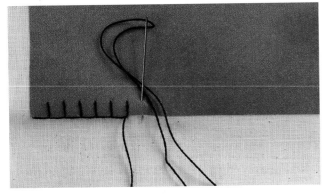

Use this stitch along the edge of appliqués or to finish the edge of a cloth. A good rule of thumb is to make the depth of the stitch as long as the distance between the stitches. When these stitches are very close together, it is called a Buttonhole Stitch.

Button Embellishments

There are so many creative embellishments in the stores, all wonderful and ready to use, but here are a few decorative variations that I like to apply on some otherwise plain and ordinary buttons. I love to cover buttons with fabric. Of course, you can buy the kits for covering buttons, but I generally sift through my bucket of buttons and find something I can recycle. You can also combine buttons with other items to make truly one-of-a-kind adornments.

Covered Shank Button

By gathering a circle of fabric over the top of a button, you can make an embellishment to match any project.

1. Glue the top of the button to a scrap of fleece. Trim the fleece to fit the button.

2. Cut out a circle about two times the diameter of the button. *Note:* If your button has a high dome shape, you may need a larger circle.

3. Finger press a narrow (⅛") hem around the edge of the fabric circle and sew a gathering stitch all around near the fold.

4. Place the fleece side of the button on the wrong side of the fabric and pull the threads to gather the fabric up and over the edge of the button, around the shank.

5. Sew the button in place. If the shank is too long or you prefer the button to be flat, snip off the shank before covering the button; then you can glue the button down.

Variations of Covered Buttons

Embroider or bead the fabric before attaching it to the button — or use scraps of old embroidered pieces for a soft vintage look.

You can also cover a flat button with holes in the same way and then use the holes in the button to sew it on.

And More Buttons ...

Stack one or two smaller buttons on top of a big button, matching the holes, and stitch it in place.

Add a button to the center of a silk flower, a fabric yo-yo, or a crocheted flower for a contrast in color and texture.

Yo-Yo Embellishments

I almost always finish a yo-yo with a button, so I am including this how-to with the button embellishments.

1. Cut a circle of fabric about two times the diameter of the desired finished size.

2. Prepare a needle with a doubled strand of matching thread with a knot at the end. Turning in a ⅛" seam allowance as you go, sew gathering stitches all around close to the folded edge.

3. Pull the stitches tightly to close the circle. (This is the same basic technique I use to cover a button — but leaving out the button.) Smooth and flatten the yo-yo so that the hole is in the center. *Note:* If the hole is too big, try using longer gathering stitches.

4. Sew a button over the hole or leave it as is. The yo-yo can be glued in place or sewn with an invisible or decorative stitch, such as a blanket stitch.

For the Love of Gardening

The colors and textures of nature and gardening are always inspirational when working with fabrics and fibers. The collection of projects here includes a gardening doll with loads of fun embellishments and a practical garden journal with a coordinating bookmark. The appliquéd sweatshirt has a folk art look and a dimensional fabric flower pin is the quickest of the set.

This doll showcases a number of simple steps I have used over the years to make a basic doll that can be used on a table or mantle. The charm is in the embellishments! In this project, the dried moss and flower hair, branch and wire rake, twig arms, button eyes and homespun fabrics all emphasize nature.

⊞ 12" tall
⏱ An evening

MATERIALS

Fabric:
- Scrap of natural muslin
- Fat quarter of gold plaid homespun
- Scrap of gold floral print
- Scrap of black and gold plaid homespun

2 cups poly pellets
Fiberfill stuffing
2 mottled cream and brown buttons, 7/16" diameter
Gold button, 5/8" diameter
10-12 small twigs, 4" long
48" length of jute
Spanish moss
Small dried flowers
Wood birdhouse, 2" x 1⅜"
Small screw eye
8" branch, ¼" diameter
18" length of 19-gauge wire

Matching sewing threads
Embroidery floss:
- Brown
- Red

Thin wire (28-32 gauge) or masking tape
Fade-out pen
Embroidery needle
Cosmetic powdered blush
Cotton-tipped swab
Fray preventative
Permanent fabric adhesive
Wire clippers
Needle nose pliers
Patterns:
- Head on page 116
- Sleeve on page 117

CUTTING INSTRUCTIONS

From the gold plaid homespun, cut:
- Two 7½" x 11½" rectangles for the body

From the gold floral print, cut:
- One 6" x 7½" rectangle for the apron

From the black and gold plaid, cut:
- One 9" x 9" square for the shawl

23

Instructions

DOLL HEAD AND BODY

1. Trace the head pattern onto the muslin.

2. Fold the muslin in half with the pattern on top.

3. Sew all around on the pattern lines, leaving the bottom edge open.

4. Cut out the shape about ⅛" from the seam. Clip the curves and turn the head right-side out.

5. Stuff the head and shoulders firmly with fiberfill; hand sew the opening closed.

6. To sew the facial features, place the beginning and ending knots at the top of the head where the hair will cover them. Using two strands of brown floss, make a ⅝"-long straight stitch down the center of the face for the nose and sew the two mottled buttons on either side of the line for the eyes. Make a small straight stitch with two strands of red floss for the mouth.

7. Rub the cotton-tipped swab onto the powdered blush and apply it to the face in a circular motion to make the cheeks. Set the head aside.

8. Pin the two body rectangles together, right sides together, and sew along the two long sides and one short end (bottom).

9. To make a "box bottom" so the doll will stand, match the bottom seam with the adjacent side seam and flatten to make a point. Pin the seams together and sew a line 1" from the point, perpendicular to the seam, through both layers. Repeat on the other side.

10. Trim the two new seam allowances to ¼".

11. Turn the body right-side out.

12. Fold in a ¾" hem at the top open end.

13. Pour the poly pellets into the bottom of the doll; stuff the remainder with fiberfill up to about 1½" from the top. Insert the head and add more fiberfill if necessary.

14. Hand sew gathering stitches around the top, ¼" from the folded edge. Pull the thread to gather the fabric snugly around the neck. Before knotting the thread, add or take out bits of fiberfill so the body is firm but not too puffy right below the neck. Knot and clip the thread.

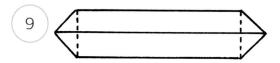

APRON

1. Apply fray preventative to the sides of the apron rectangle and let it dry.

2. Fold a 1" hem on one 6" side and hand sew gathering stitches ¾" from the fold. Pull the thread until the apron measures 3" across; knot and clip the thread.

3. Apply glue to the back of the apron along the gathers and press it to the front of the body with the bottom of the apron 1½" above the bottom of the doll.

4. Cut a 36" length from the jute and wrap it around the body, covering the gathers of the apron. Tie a bow in the center front and trim any excess. Tie a knot at each end of the jute.

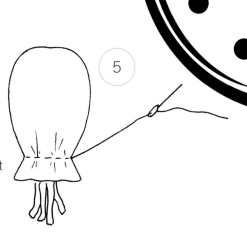

ARMS AND HANDS

1. Divide the 4" twigs into two bundles. Wrap each bundle with the thin wire or masking tape, leaving 2" free for the hands. Set the twigs aside.

2. Trace the sleeve pattern two times on the wrong side of the gold plaid homespun. Fold the fabric in half, right sides together, with the pattern on top and sew on the pattern lines, leaving the sleeves open at the bottom.

3. Cut out each sleeve ⅛" from the seam; clip the curves and turn right-side out.

4. Fold and press a 1" hem at the bottom of each sleeve and hand sew gathering stitches all around, ¾" from the fold. Do not knot or clip the thread.

5. Push some fiberfill into the top of one sleeve and insert a twig bundle far enough so that only about 1" extends below. Add more fiberfill to shape the arms. Pull on the thread to gather the sleeve tightly around the twigs; knot and clip the thread. Repeat to make a second arm.

6. Glue the back of the sleeves to the front shoulder of the doll.

HAIR

1. Glue Spanish moss to the head.

2. Apply glue to the flowers and insert them into the moss until the head is covered.

SHAWL

1. Fringe the edges of the black and gold square ¼".

2. Fold the square in half diagonally. Fold the diagonal side again about ¾" and wrap the shawl around the doll's neck, crossing the ends at the center front.

3. Sew the gold button through the ends of the shawl to hold them in place.

RAKE

1. Wrap one end of the 19-gauge wire around the end of the branch several times. Shape the wire into five irregular prongs with your fingers. Hold the wire with the needle nose pliers where you would like to bend the wire and pull the wire with your other hand. Bring the wire back to the branch and wrap it around the end again to hold it.

2. Glue the rake to one arm in front of the doll.

FINISHING TOUCHES

1. Attach the screw eye to the top of the birdhouse.

2. Insert the remaining jute through the screw eye; tie the ends in a knot about 3" above the birdhouse.

3. Glue the knot to the other hand, under the gathered end of the sleeve.

Garden Journal

A garden journal is a very useful tool to keep track of what you planted, how it grew and any other notes and pictures that will give you guidance and inspiration for the next season. This journal cover is a simple design of fused appliqués on raw-edged backgrounds with just a minimal amount of hand stitching. The coordinating bookmark tag is embroidered with the title and has a beautiful ribbon and bead tail for marking your page.

8" x 6"

2 hours

MATERIALS

Fabric:
- Scrap of natural osnaburg
- Scraps of assorted prints in green, orange, red, gold and brown for the appliqués
- Scrap of green solid

8" x 6" spiral bound journal

Scrap of fleece

³⁄₁₆" metal eyelet

24" length of green ribbon, ³⁄₈" wide

Large green bead or shank button, about ¾" diameter

Black embroidery floss

Tan sewing thread

Fusible adhesive

Fade-out pen

Embroidery needle

Embroidery hoop

Eyelet setting tool

Permanent fabric adhesive

Patterns:
- Carrot with Top on page 118
- Flower with Leaf on page 116
- Tree Branch with Leaves on page 117
- "garden journal" Embroidery Pattern on page 116
- Tag on page 117

CUTTING INSTRUCTIONS

From the natural osnaburg, cut:
- One 2½" x 3¼" rectangle
- One 3¼" x 3¼" square
- One 6" x 1¾" rectangle

From the green solid, cut:
- One 7" x 5½" rectangle

Instructions

1. Arrange the three osnaburg shapes on the green rectangle with the long piece on the bottom and the other two centered above it; pin the shapes in place.

2. Use two strands of black embroidery floss to attach the shapes with a running stitch ⅛" from the edges.

3. Trace all the appliqué patterns onto the paper side of the fusible adhesive, leaving a margin of at least ½" between the shapes.

4. Cut the shapes apart, but do not cut on the pattern lines.

5. Follow the manufacturer's instructions to iron the shapes to the wrong side of the selected appliqué fabrics.

6. Cut out the shapes on the pattern lines. Remove the paper backings.

7. Arrange the appliqué shapes in the three osnaburg backgrounds. When you are satisfied with the arrangement, iron the appliqués in place. *Note:* In my sample, I placed the carrot diagonally in the 2½" x 3¼" rectangle with the top overlapping the edge. I centered the flower in the square and the tree branch is centered in the bottom strip.

8. Glue the green rectangle to the front of the journal.

9. Trace the tag pattern onto the remaining osnaburg and trace the title "garden journal" in the center of the tag shape (leave enough fabric for the back of the tag).

10. Place the fabric in an embroidery hoop. Backstitch over the lines using two strands of black floss.

11. Cut out the tag. Use the tag pattern to cut out a backing.

12. Hold the tag front and back together, right sides together, and pin to the fleece. Sew all around with ¼" seam allowance, leaving a 2" opening along one side for turning.

13. Trim the corners and turn the tag right-side out. Fold in the seam allowance and hand sew the opening closed.

14. Top stitch ¼" from the edges with tan thread.

15. Using the eyelet setter, follow the manufacturer's instructions to insert the eyelet ½" from the end of the tag.

16. Fold the ribbon in half and insert the looped end through the eyelet, front to back. Thread the ends through the loop and pull to attach the ribbon to the tag.

17. Thread the ribbon ends through the large bead or through the shank of the button. Tie a knot at the bottom to hold the bead or button in place; trim any excess ribbon. *Note:* Be sure the ribbon is long enough so that the tag rests at the top of the journal and the bead hangs below.

Appliquéd Sweatshirt

This sweatshirt project is an example of a raw edge appliqué technique. The shapes are held in place with lightweight fusible adhesive, but the stitching is decorative and does not cover the edges of the fabric, giving the design a casual look.

▭ Adult-size sweatshirt
🕐 1½ hours

MATERIALS

Fabric:
- Scraps of assorted prints in greens, rusts, gold and ecru for the appliqués

Prewashed sweatshirt (The model is "yam" color with boxer bottom. See Resources for details.)

Fusible adhesive

Coordinating sewing threads (See Tip)
Patterns:
- Flower 1 on page 118
- Flower 2 on page 119
- Flower 3 on page 118

Vary the look of the appliqués with thread colors and stitches. For example, machine stitch near the edges with a straight stitch, a small zigzag stitch or a decorative stitch. Use thread that matches or contrasts with the fabrics or use a black topstitch weight for a bolder stitch.

Instructions

1. Trace all the patterns onto the paper side of the fusible adhesive, leaving a margin of at least ½" between the shapes.

2. Cut the shapes apart but do not cut on the pattern lines.

3. Follow the manufacturer's directions to iron the adhesive to the wrong side of the selected appliqué fabrics.

4. Cut out the shapes on the pattern lines. Remove the paper backing.

5. Arrange the stems, flowers, flower centers and leaves on the front of the sweatshirt. When you are satisfied with the arrangement, iron the appliqués in place. *Note:* In my sample, I placed the bottoms of the stems 6" above the bottom edge of the sweatshirt.

6. Finish the appliqué pieces by machine stitching near the edges. Use green thread to straight stitch on the stems and to sew a short zigzag stitch around the leaves. Use ecru thread to straight stitch around the daisy petals and rust-colored thread to zigzag stitch around all the other flower parts. Pull the beginning and ending threads to the inside of the sweatshirt and tie them off. Clip the threads ¼" from the knot.

7. Press the appliqués again to secure the bond.

Tip

To launder a fused appliqué wearable such as this sweatshirt, turn it inside out before putting it in the washer and use a gentle cycle. Hang it to dry or use a low heat setting on the dryer. Press the appliqués.

Fabric Flower Pin

This flower is so easy to make that you will want one to match every coat in your closet … and hat and tote and sweater, too. The construction is a variation of a method used in making the beautiful old Victorian ribbon flowers. The flower center is a covered button.

3¾" diameter flower

1 hour

Besides using this flower as a pin, you could make several to decorate a grapevine wreath or a basket, design a quilted wall hanging with dimensional flowers, or attach the flowers to long stems and fill a vase.

MATERIALS

Fabric:
- ⅛ yd. red print
- Scrap of green print
- Scrap of gold print
- Scrap of green felt

Shank button, 1¼" diameter

3" piece of chenille stem

Pin back

Matching sewing threads

Permanent fabric adhesive

Fade-out pen or fine-line marker

Patterns:
- U-Stitching Guide on page 117
- Flower Center on page 119
- Leaf on page 116

CUTTING INSTRUCTIONS

From the red print, cut:
- One 4" x 21¼" strip for the flower

From the green print, cut:
- One 2" x 3½" strip for the stem

Instructions

1. Fold and press the red fabric strip in half lengthwise, wrong sides together.

2. Make five "U-gathers" to form the petals of the flower. To start, use the U-stitch pattern to make five stitching guides along the fabric strip, starting and ending 1" from the ends and with the fold at the top. Leave about ⅛" between the stitching lines of each segment.

3. Using doubled thread, hand sew gathering stitches on the pattern lines. When moving from one "U" to the next, go over the edge of the fabric fold and back into the pattern.

4. After each section is stitched, pull on the thread to gather the fabric into a petal.

5. When all the petals are formed, knot the thread and then use the same thread to sew the ends together in a seam, shaping the petals into a round flower.

6. Using the Flower Center pattern, follow the Button Embellishments instructions on page 17 to cover the shank button for the flower center. Glue the button to the center of the flower.

7. Press a ½" hem on one short side of the green stem fabric.

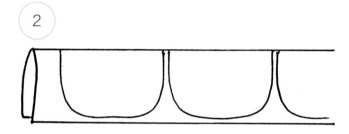

2

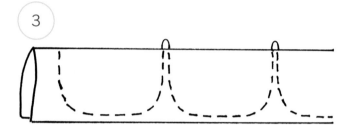

3

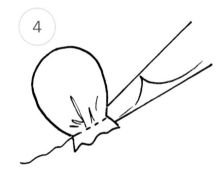

4

8. Place the chenille stem on one side of the green strip with the end tucked inside the folded hem and roll the green stem fabric around it. Fold a hem under at the end and glue the end down to hold it in place. Curve the stem slightly and glue the unhemmed end to the back of the flower.

9. Trace the leaf pattern onto the wrong side of the remaining green print. Fold the fabric in half with the pattern on top.

10. Stitch around the leaf on the pattern lines, leaving the bottom open.

11. Cut out ⅛" from the seam of the leaf; clip the curves and trim the tip. Turn it right-side out.

12. Fold a pleat in the center of the leaf at the open end; use a dot of glue to hold it in place. Glue the end of the leaf to the back of the flower.

13. Cut out a circle of felt large enough to cover the raw edges on the back of the flower.

14. Glue the felt circle to the back of the flower.

15. Sew or glue the pin back to the felt circle.

The Gift of Friendship

What a wonderful way to let someone know that you appreciate their friendship — a decorated gift basket lined with crisp red and white fabrics and wrapped with an embroidered mini quilt. The felt and fabric heart ornament can adorn the basket and be used later as a holiday decoration. The card expresses the warm feelings of friendship with paper, fabric and embellishments.

A gift basket can be almost as much fun to plan and fill as it is to receive. Choose an appropriate theme and gather items that accentuate it. A gourmet basket for your tasteful friend for example, might have breads, jams, teas or special blend coffees, chocolates and maybe a few unusual kitchen tools and a cookbook. Use strips of fabric for bows and add the recipe if you include homemade goodies. Perhaps a basket of scented bath supplies and a pretty towel, or a garden theme with tools, gloves, seeds, bulbs and a good planting guide would be the right combination. A friend is a very special gift, deserving of a very special gift basket!

A sweet mini quilt wraps around a basket with long red ribbons. The sentiment is embroidered with red floss and framed with red print fabrics and white buttons.

 11" x 4½"

⏱ An evening

MATERIALS

Fabric:
- Scrap of white solid
- ¼ yd. red-and-white plaid
- Scrap of dark red check
- Scrap of white with red print

Batting

3⅔ yd. red grosgrain ribbon, 1" wide

4 white buttons, ¾" diameter

Red embroidery floss

Matching sewing threads

White quilting thread for hand quilting

Fade-out pen

Embroidery needle

Embroidery hoop

Hand quilting needle

Patterns:
- "Friendship" Embroidery Pattern on page 120
- Heart Quilting Pattern on page 120

CUTTING INSTRUCTIONS

From the white solid, cut:
- One 10½" x 7" rectangle

From the red-and-white plaid, cut:
- Two 1½" x 3" outer border strips
- Two 1½" x 11½" top and bottom border strips
- One 11½" x 5" rectangle for the backing

From the dark red check, cut:
- Two 1" x 3" inner border strips

From the white with red print, cut:
- Two 1½" x 3" middle border strips

From the batting, cut:
- One 11½" x 5" rectangle

Instructions

Note: This mini quilt fits a 35"-40"-diameter basket; adjust the ribbon lengths to fit your own basket.

1. Transfer the word "Friendship" to the center of the white solid rectangle using the fade-out pen.

2. Place the white solid fabric in an embroidery hoop and backstitch over the pattern lines using two strands of red embroidery floss. Make French knots for the dots (see page 16 for French knot instructions).

3. Trim the embroidered white fabric to a 6½" x 3" rectangle, centering the embroidered word.

4. Sew the 1"-wide inner border strips to the sides of the embroidered block; press the seams outward.

5. Sew the 1½"-wide middle border strips to the inner border strips; press the seams outward.

6. Sew the 3"-long outer border strips to the middle borders; press the seams outward.

7. Sew the 11½"-long top and bottom border strips to the top and bottom of the block; press the seams outward.

8. Place the batting on your work surface, smoothing it out with your hands. Place the backing, right-side up, on top of the batting. Cover it with the pieced and embroidered top, right-side down.

9. Sew all around with a ¼" seam, leaving a 3" opening along one edge for turning.

10. Clip the corners and trim the seam allowance of the batting close to the seam. Turn the mini quilt right-side out.

11. Fold in the seam allowance on the opening and hand sew the opening closed.

12. Using the hand quilting thread and quilting needle, quilt by "stitching in the ditch" (very close to the seam line) between each border and between the borders and the embroidered block. Quilt stitches are small, even running stitches going through all the layers of the piece. This step can also be done by machine.

13. Center the heart quilting pattern on the embroidered block. Draw around it with the fade-out pen.

14. Quilt by hand directly on the line, slipping the needle under the floss when the heart intersects the embroidered letters.

15. Cut the ribbon in half (each length will be about 66" long). Place one ribbon on your work surface and lay the mini quilt right-side up on the ribbon so 14" extends on the right side and about 44" extends on the left side. Attach the ribbon to the quilt by sewing a button to each top corner, sewing all the way through the ribbon. Repeat this step on the bottom, but reverse the ribbon lengths so the longer end is on the right and the shorter is on the left.

16. Wrap the long ribbon ends around the basket and tie bows on each side of the mini quilt.

Fabric-Lined Basket

Lining a gift basket with cheery fabric is an easy but effective way to dress it up. The ruffles and lining are simple tubes of fabric gathered to fit the sides of the basket and the bottom is padded with batting and fabric.

5½" tall
2 hours

MATERIALS

Fabric:
- ⅓ yd. white with red print
- ¾ yd. dark red check

Basket with handle and straight sides (the sample is 5½" high and 37½" in circumference)

Batting

Cardboard to fit the bottom of the basket

Matching sewing threads

Heavy-duty thread or fine crochet cord

Piece of tissue paper

Permanent fabric adhesive

CUTTING INSTRUCTIONS

From the white with red print, cut:
- 5" x (two times the circumference of the basket — See Steps 1 and 2)

From the dark red check, cut:
- (inside height + 2") x (two times the circumference — See Steps 1 and 3)

Instructions

1. Measure the height of your basket on the inside. Measure all around the basket for the circumference.

2. To determine the dimensions for the white and red ruffle, you will need a 5"-wide strip that is equal to two times the basket's circumference. Seam two strips together if necessary to reach that measurement. (The sample requires two 5" x 37½" strips, sewn together.)

3. To determine the dimensions of the dark red checked lining, add 2" to the inside height of the basket and use the same length as needed for the ruffle. (The sample requires two 7" x 37½" strips, sewn together.)

4. Sew the short ends of the ruffle strips together to form a tube.

5. Fold the ruffle tube in half lengthwise, wrong sides together, and press.

6. To gather the ruffle, refer to Zigzag Gathers on page 13. Place the heavy thread on the fabric, ½" from the raw edges. Sew all around, leaving a few inches of heavy thread free at each end.

7. Pull the thread to gather the ruffle to fit the inside of the basket rim (leave it slightly loose as it is easy to fit in a little excess fabric when gluing). Tie the ends together and clip the excess thread. Adjust the gathers evenly around the tube.

8. Apply glue to a few inches of the gathering line on the wrong side (where the heavy thread lies) of the ruffle and press this to the inside top edge of the basket. The top edge of the ruffle should extend 1½" above the basket. Continue to glue the ruffle around the basket, a few inches at a time.

9. Sew the short ends of the lining together to form a tube.

10. Fold down a 1" hem along one end and press.

11. Use the zigzag stitch over heavy thread to make a gathering line ¾" from the top fold and again ½" from the raw edge at the bottom on the wrong side of the tube.

12. Pull the threads to fit the tube to the inside of the basket; knot the ends together (leave it slightly loose as it is easy to fit in a little excess fabric when gluing).

13. Adjust the gathers evenly and place the lining inside the basket with the right side showing. Apply glue to the top gathered line on the wrong side of the liner, just a few inches at a time, and press it to the gather line on the ruffle. The top of the liner should be about 1¼" down from the top of the ruffle.

14. Apply glue to the bottom of the basket along the edge and pull the lining straight down, pressing the edge into the glue. Work a small section at a time.

15. To make a pattern for the padded basket bottom, place the tissue paper inside the basket, pushing it to the edge and draw around the side with a pencil. Remove the paper, cut out the circle, and use the pattern to cut the cardboard. Place the cardboard inside the basket to check for fit, and trim if necessary.

16. Cut a piece of fabric 1" larger all around than the cardboard and cut a piece of batting to fit the cardboard.

17. Glue the batting to one side of the cardboard.

18. Hand sew gathering stitches around the edge of the fabric for the bottom.

19. Place the cardboard, batting side down, on the wrong side of the fabric. Pull the stitches so the fabric pulls snugly over the edge of the cardboard.

20. Apply glue to the inside bottom of the basket; insert the padded bottom, pressing it down firmly to adhere. Do not apply the glue to the padded bottom itself, because the glue may touch the lining as it is pushed down.

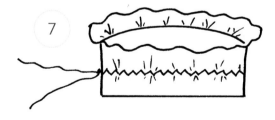

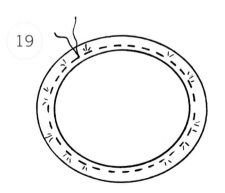

This little ornament can decorate the gift basket, the Christmas tree or even an arrangement of budding branches for Valentine's Day. It is made of felt with a fabric insert and just enough glass beads to dress it up!

▭▭▭ 4½" x 3¾"

⏱ 1½ hours

MATERIALS

Fabric:
- Scrap of red-and-white plaid
- 9" x 12" sheet of red felt

Scrap of fusible adhesive

Scrap of fusible lightweight interfacing

White button, ½" diameter

About 55 red glass beads, size 6/0

12" length of white grosgrain ribbon, ¼" wide

Fiberfill stuffing

Embroidery floss:
- White
- Red

Red beading or quilting thread

Beading or quilting needle

Permanent fabric adhesive

Patterns:
- Heart Ornament on page 120
- Fabric Insert on page 120

Instructions

1. Use the heart ornament pattern to cut two hearts from the red felt. Cut out the inside heart from *only one* of the felt hearts for the front of the ornament.

2. Follow the manufacturer's instructions to fuse a small (at least 4½" x 3") piece of interfacing to the wrong side of plaid fabric. Cut out the fabric insert from this piece using the fabric insert pattern.

3. Using three strands of white embroidery floss, sew a blanket stitch around the edges of the heart cutout.

4. Apply glue to the edge of the cutout opening on the wrong side; place the opening over the plaid heart. Press the edges down to glue the pieces together.

5. Sew the button to the felt heart above the cutout.

6. Pin the felt heart back and front wrong sides together. Fold the ribbon in half and insert the folded end at the top of the heart between the layers. Blanket stitch the edges together with three strands of red floss, catching the ribbon in the stitches. Before closing, pad the heart lightly with stuffing.

7. To add the beads, knot a strand of beading or quilting thread and slip the needle between the layers. Come out at the end of a blanket stitch. Add a bead and go back into the felt. Repeat the step so the bead is sewn on with two stitches. Come out at the next blanket stitch and sew on another bead. Continue around the ornament, using the blanket stitches as a guide for the placement of the beads.

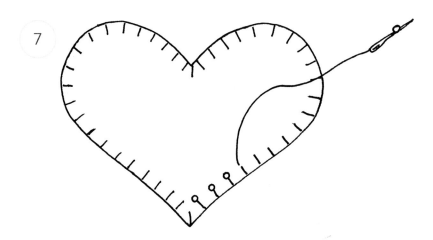

Fabric and paper in the same project makes a great combination. This card has lots of other interesting features too — a vinyl pocket, metal charms, beautiful fibers and a sweet, rubber-stamped sentiment.

▭ 5½" x 4¼"
⏱ 1 hour

MATERIALS

Fabric:
- Scrap of red-and-white plaid
- Scrap of dark red check

5½" x 4¼" red folded card (or red cardstock cut and folded to that size)

Cardstock:
- Black
- White

Scrap of sheet music

Scrap of clear vinyl

Rubber stamp with friendship quote

Black pigment ink

Clear embossing powder

Red eyelet, ¼" diameter

3 assorted red and black fibers or narrow ribbons, 8" long

2 assorted silver music charms, ¾" – 1¼" long

Black sewing thread

Scrap of fusible adhesive

Heat gun for embossing

Eyelet setter

Craft glue

Patterns:
- Heart Quilting Pattern on page 120
- Small Heart Appliqué on page 120

Instructions

1. Cut a 4¼" x 3" rectangle from the sheet music. *Note:* Photocopy the sheet music onto a piece of white cardstock if you do not want to cut the sheet music itself.

2. Cut a 3¼" x 2" piece of clear vinyl; center it on the sheet music. Sew along the sides and bottom of the vinyl with black thread, forming a pocket. Pull the threads to the back of the paper and tie the ends.

3. Glue the sheet music to the front of the card.

4. Stamp the friendship quote on a piece of white cardstock. Immediately cover the quote with embossing powder; shake off the excess. Heat the powder with the heat gun until it melts and raises.

5. Trim the cardstock to 4¼" x 1¾", centering the quote.

6. Cut a 5½" x 2⅛" rectangle from black cardstock. Center the quote on the rectangle and attach it by sewing down each side with black thread.

7. Glue the cardstock to the inside of the card.

8. Apply a 2½" x 2" piece of fusible adhesive to the wrong side of the dark red check fabric. Remove the paper backing and fold the fabric over to cover the adhesive. Fuse the layers together.

9. Use the pattern to cut a heart from the dark red check fabric.

10. Punch a hole at the upper right edge of the heart with the eyelet tool and insert the red eyelet. Follow the manufacturer's instructions to set the eyelet.

11. Fold the black and red fibers in half and push the folded end through the eyelet in the heart. Insert the fiber ends through the loop and pull to tighten the loop around the fibers.

12. Attach the music charm to the fibers using a needle and thread.

13. Insert the heart into the vinyl pocket at an angle.

14. Draw the small heart pattern onto the paper side of the fusible adhesive; cut out about ¼" from the lines. Iron the adhesive to the wrong side of the red-and-white plaid fabric.

15. Cut out the heart and remove the paper backing. Iron the heart to the inside of the card beside the quote.

16. Glue the remaining charm on the heart appliqué.

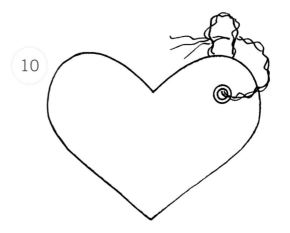

Curl Up with a Good Book

When the weather outside is cold and dreary, a good book and comfy surroundings are too inviting to resist. A patchwork flannel throw and soft pillow set the mood with style and comfort. An old lamp, made new again with flannel prints and trims, and a couple of charming bookmarks complete the set.

A few facts about sewing with flannel ...
- Use only good-quality flannel, sometimes sold as "quilter's flannel," for your home décor projects. It has more body, is easier to sew, stretches and pills less, and feels softer. It is definitely worth the higher price.
- Flannel has a soft, fuzzy nap, and the texture of flannel actually helps to hold the layers in place, so you can pin less (and save time!).
- I preshrink flannel if I am using it for clothing, but for throws and quilts, I use a cotton batting and let the layers shrink together for an old-fashioned look.

Patchwork Flannel Throw

The pattern for this cozy throw is so simple — big squares with a handful of four-patch blocks added for contrast. Using a variety of coordinated colors and prints gives ordinary patchwork a real punch. Instead of quilting, the layers are held together with assorted buttons, a quick but effective way to finish this snuggly blanket.

▥ 40" square
⏱ An evening

MATERIALS

Flannel fabric:
- 6 assorted fat quarters of coordinating prints in green, lavender and beige for the patchwork
- 1¼ yd. flannel print for the backing

40½" square cotton batting

16 assorted green and beige buttons, ⅞" diameter
Matching sewing threads
Heavy-duty thread to match the buttons
25 safety pins, medium size

CUTTING INSTRUCTIONS

From the assorted flannel prints, cut:
- 20 (8½") squares
- 20 (4½") squares

From the flannel backing fabric, cut:
- One 40½" square

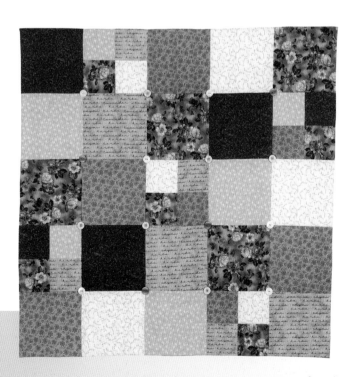

Instructions

1. Divide the 20 small squares into five sets of four squares each. Arrange each set of squares into a four-patch block: two rows of two squares each.

2. Sew the two squares of each row together, and then sew the two rows together to make each set into an 8½" block.

3. Arrange all the blocks (the four-patch blocks and solid blocks) into five rows of five blocks each, with one four-patch block in each row.

4. Sew the blocks together in each row. Press the seams to one side, reversing the direction for each row.

5. Pin the rows together, matching the seam lines. Pressing the seams in opposite directions makes it easier to keep the seam lines in place. Sew the rows together to make a 40½" pieced top.

6. Place the batting on your work surface, smoothing it out with your hands. Place the backing right-side up on top of the batting and cover it with the pieced top, right-side down.

7. Sew all around with a ¼" seam, leaving a 6" opening along one edge for turning.

8. Clip the corners and trim the seam allowance of the batting close to the seam. Turn the throw right-side out.

9. Fold in the seam allowance on the opening and hand sew the opening closed. Press all around the edges.

10. To hold the layers together for finishing, insert a safety pin in each square, all the way through to the back.

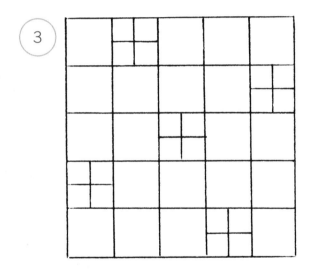

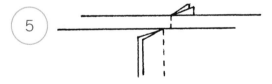

11. Use heavy-duty thread to sew a button to each intersection of the 8" blocks, sewing through all layers. Remove the safety pins.

Flannel Pillow

This pillow is basically a tube of fabric pulled over a purchased pillow form. The contrasting flannel prints and large covered buttons give it personality. One side has snaps under the buttons so the pillow case can be removed for washing.

24½" x 12"

1½ hours

MATERIALS

Flannel fabrics:
- ½ yd. each of two coordinating prints for the pillowcase
- Scrap of contrasting print for the covered buttons

Scrap of fleece

12" x 16" pillow form

4 shank buttons, 1⅜" diameter

2 large snap sets

Matching sewing threads

No-fray solution

Permanent fabric adhesive

CUTTING INSTRUCTIONS

From one flannel print, cut:
- One 25" x 17" rectangle for the center panel

From the coordinating flannel print, cut:
- Two 25" x 8½" rectangles for borders

From contrasting flannel print, cut:
- Four 2¾" circles for the button covers

Instructions

1. Press under a ¼" hem along one long edge of each border strip; press under ¼" again for a doubled hem.

2. Sew the remaining long edge of each border to a 25" side of the center panel; press the seams toward the borders.

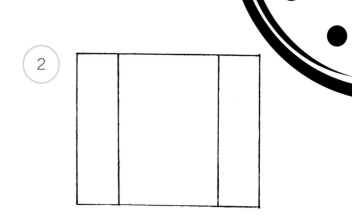

3. Fold the pieced rectangle in half lengthwise with the right sides together. Open the pressed hems at each end and sew the seam from end to end to make a tube.

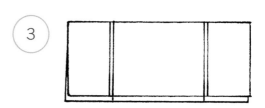

4. Re-press the hems at the ends and sew in place.

5. Fold under 3¼" on each border and press. The borders should now measure 4" wide.

6. Apply no-fray solution to the edge of each flannel circle; let dry.

7. Glue a scrap of fleece to the top of each button and trim the fleece to fit.

8. Refer to the Button Embellishments instructions on page 17 to make four flannel-covered buttons. Knot the thread, but do not clip it.

9. Slip the pillow form inside the flannel case until it is in the center.

10. Using the thread still attached to the buttons, sew two buttons to the border on one side of the pillow, 1½" from the outer edge and 3½" from the top and bottom. Sew through all layers.

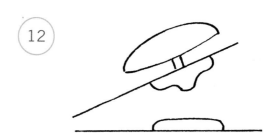

11. On the other side of the pillow, measure the same positions for the buttons, but sew a snap set inside the pillow case.

12. Sew a button on top of each snap on the front of the pillow.

Flannel-Covered Lamp

You won't find a lamp like this at your local furniture store! Recycle the ugly lamp in the attic with a flannel cover tied over the base and a flannel print and trims glued to the old shade.

▭ Custom
🕐 2 hours

MATERIALS

Flannel fabrics:
- 1 yd. print for the base and shade
- ⅔ yd. coordinating print for the base lining

Small lamp (the sample has a 7"-high base, not including the hardware, and a 7"-high shade; adjust yardage for a different size lamp)

⅔ yd. fleece

1½ yd. tan braided cord, ½" diameter

1½ yd. tan gimp trim, ½" wide

Matching sewing threads

No-fray solution

Spray adhesive

Permanent fabric adhesive

2 large pieces of paper or double pages from a newspaper for the pattern

String

Marker

Thumbtack

LAMP BASE INSTRUCTIONS

1. Measure the lamp base from the top edge on one side, down and under the lamp and up to the top edge on the opposite side. Add 6" to this measurement for the diameter of the circle needed.

Ex: The sample requires a 24" circle (7" + 4" + 7" + 6").

2. Fold one large sheet of paper in half and in half again. Tie one end of the string around the marker. From the marker, measure one-half of the diameter determined in Step 1 and insert the thumbtack through the string at this point. Place the thumbtack at the folded corner of the paper and swing the marker from one edge of the paper to the other, making a quarter-circle pattern.

3. Cut out on the line; unfold the paper. The circle created is the pattern for the lamp base cover.

4. Use the pattern to cut a circle from each flannel print and one from the fleece.

5. Layer the circles with the fleece on the bottom and the two prints right sides together on top of the fleece; pin through all the layers.

6. Sew all around the edge, leaving a 6" opening for turning. Trim the fleece close to the seam line and clip the curves. Turn right-side out and press.

7. Fold in the seam allowance on the opening and hand sew the opening closed with small stitches.

8. Topstitch all around, using different colors of thread in the top and bobbin to match the base cover and lining.

9. Place the lamp base in the center of the cover and mark the spot where the lamp cord extends from the lamp.

10. Machine stitch a buttonhole on the marked spot, long enough so the head of the plug can pass through. *Note:* If you prefer, you can cut a slit through all the layers of the cover. Apply no-fray solution to the edges and let dry. Hand sew a blanket stitch all around the cut edges to make a buttonhole.

11. To cover the lamp, place the base in the center of the circle on the lining side. Pull the cord through the buttonhole and bring the edges of the fabric up near the top of the lamp. Wrap the braided cord around the fabric and tie it in a bow in the front. Tie a knot in each end of the cord. Apply no-fray solution liberally to the cut ends and let dry.

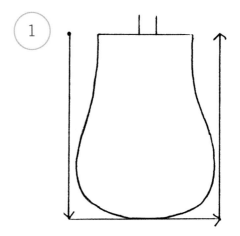

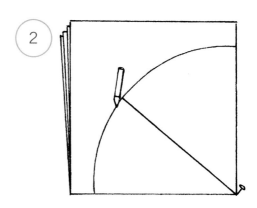

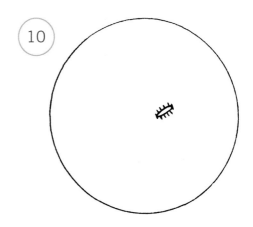

LAMP SHADE INSTRUCTIONS

1. To make a pattern for the shade, place the seam of the lamp shade ½" from the edge of the remaining paper. Slowly roll the shade across the paper, marking the paper along both the bottom and the top edge of the shade as it moves. Stop when you reach the seam again. Add ½" to the top and bottom lines and cut out the pattern.

2. Use the pattern to cut one lamp shade cover from the flannel print.

3. Spray adhesive on the shade and place one straight end of the fabric at the seam line of the shade with ½" of fabric extending at the top and bottom. Smooth the fabric onto the shade, moving around the shade and keeping the ½" margin even. You may wish to just spray a section of the shade at a time. Overlap the beginning edge at the back and fold the excess fabric under; glue the edge down.

4. Fold the excess top fabric to the inside of the shade and glue in place with permanent fabric adhesive.

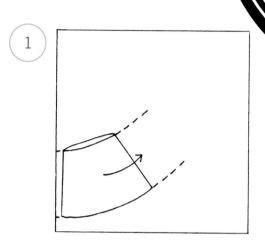

5. Fold and glue the excess bottom fabric to the inside of the shade.

6. Starting at the back seam, glue the gimp trim to the bottom edge of the shade. Cut off the excess gimp, leaving a ½" hem to turn under and glue down.

7. In the same manner, glue the gimp trim to the top of the shade.

Flannel Bookmarks

Use a few scraps from your sewing projects to make these unique bookmarks. Iron-on adhesive gives body to the tag shapes and seals the raw edges. Beads, charms, ribbons and buttons add the fun.

3" x 6½"

1 hour for each bookmark

MATERIALS   (for both bookmarks)

Flannel fabrics:
- Scraps of four prints

Fusible adhesive

Pattern:
- Bookmark Tag on page 121

Bookmark Tag

INSTRUCTIONS

1. Cut out a 3½" x 7" piece of fusible adhesive.

2. Follow the manufacturer's instructions to apply the piece of fusible adhesive to the wrong side of one flannel print. Remove the paper backing and fold the flannel in half with the adhesive in the middle. Press to fuse the layers together.

3. Use the bookmark tag pattern to cut a bookmark tag from the doubled flannel.

Shopping for Embellishments

When you are looking for unique embellishments for your sewing projects, don't forget to shop the scrapbooking aisles. There are many interesting items there, such as these die-cut metal letters that can be glued or sewn to your item. The bookmark would be a charming gift with a name spelled out with letter cut-outs or tiles.

Bead and Ribbon Bookmark

MATERIALS

Bookmark tag
Embroidery floss in coordinating color
Silver eyelet with ¼"-diameter hole
10" length of wire-edged ribbon, ⅝" wide
12" length of silver-colored wire, 22 gauge

Beads:
- 5 glass tubes, 8mm x 12mm
- 8 silver rounds, 6mm

Embroidery needle
Hole punch, ¼"
Eyelet setting tool
Needle nose pliers

INSTRUCTIONS

1. Using four strands of embroidery floss, blanket stitch all around the bookmark tag.

2. Punch a hole at the top of the tag about ½" down. Insert the silver eyelet and follow the manufacturer's instructions to set the eyelet.

3. Fold the silver-colored wire in half; push the looped end through the eyelet from front to back. Slip the loose wire ends through the loop and pull until the loop fits snugly against the top of the tag.

4. Fold the ribbon in half; attach it to the tag in the same manner, covering the wire loop. Trim the ribbon ends in a V-cut.

5. Place a few beads on one wire; use the pliers to curl the wire two times.

6. Add more beads above the two curls. Bend the wire into a tight curl at the end so the beads will not slip off.

7. Repeat Steps 5 and 6 with the other wire.

"read" Bookmark

MATERIALS

Bookmark tag
7" piece of green wire-edged ribbon, 7/8" wide
Shank button, 7/8" diameter
Scrap of fleece
Silver heart charm, 3/4" wide

Die-cut metal letters to spell "read," 5/8"
Matching sewing threads
Permanent fabric adhesive
Pattern:
- Bookmark Center on page 121

INSTRUCTIONS

1. Draw the bookmark center pattern onto the paper side of fusible adhesive. Apply it to the wrong side of a contrasting flannel print.

2. Cut out the pattern on the pattern lines; remove the paper backing.

3. Iron the bookmark center to the bookmark tag.

4. Cut the ribbon in half. To make each ribbon leaf, fold a ribbon length in half so the halves are side by side. Pull the wire from the two inner edges to gather the ribbon up the middle. Twist the wire ends together.

5. Wrap the excess wire around the raw edges of the ribbon or use a needle and thread to pull the ends together. Pinch the tips of the leaves to shape them.

6. To make the flannel "flower," cut a 7/8"-diameter circle from the fleece and glue it to the top of the shank button.

7. Cut a 2" circle from a contrasting color of flannel. Refer to the Covered Buttons instructions on page 17 to cover the shank button with the flannel.

8. Glue the leaves to the bookmark at the top of the center strip.

9. Glue the button between the leaves.

10. Glue the heart charm under the button.

11. Evenly space and glue the metal letters down the center front of the tag.

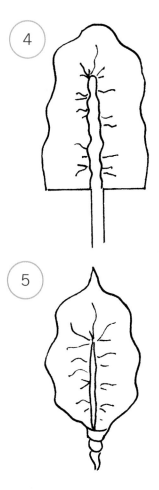

Picture This

Everyone loves to have photos of family, friends, pets and events, but what to do with them all? Here are a few suggestions using fabric and embellishments to cover photo albums and purchased frames. It's a fun adventure to find the fabrics and trims to coordinate with the photos you want to spotlight.

Covering a purchased photo album with batting and fabric is a quick and easy process. The interesting elements in these two samples are the photo transfer mini quilts and the coordinating trims. The inkjet-printable sheets are simple to use, and if you don't have a color printer, an office supply store can print them for you. They can be sewn just like any fabric and the album you create will be truly one-of-a-kind!

🗝 8⅜" x 13⅜"
⏱ An evening

"Snips and Snails" Album

To select fabrics to coordinate with your photo, consider the colors of the clothing, hair and background and the mood you wish to feature. On the boys' album, I used a photo of my two grinning grandsons and matched the plaid and blue dot to the photo. I selected a cowboy motif fabric for the album and added cording to look like a lasso and a leather sheriff badge. My three granddaughters were all dressed in pink; the girly-girl pink-and-black fabrics emphasized that look. I added pretty buttons and a ribbon, flower and beads for trims for the girls' version of a covered album.

MATERIALS

Fabric:
- ⅔ yd. cowboy motif novelty print for the album
- Scrap of dark blue dot
- Fat eighth or ¼ yd. plaid homespun

3-ring photo album, 8⅜" x 13⅜"

Inkjet-printable fabric sheet

6" x 4" color photo

Batting

6 blue buttons, ¹³⁄₁₆" diameter

1½ yd. twisted cord trim

Wood or leather sheriff badge cutout, 2¾" across

Metallic gold acrylic paint

2 pieces of lightweight cardboard to fit the covers of the album (a shirt or gift box works well)

Matching sewing threads

Scanner with inkjet color printer

Small paintbrush

Fray preventative

Permanent fabric adhesive

CUTTING INSTRUCTIONS

From the cowboy print, cut:
- One rectangle for the album cover (See Step 1)
- Two rectangles for the inside cover (See Step 9)
- Two 2½" x 12⅜" strips for the inside of the album

From the dark blue dot, cut:
- Two 1" x 4⅜" strips for the side borders of the photo quilt
- Two 1" x 7¼" strips for the top and bottom border of photo quilt

From the plaid homespun, cut:
- Two 2½" x 7¼" strips for the outer top and bottom borders of the photo quilt
- One 7¼" x 9⅜" rectangle for the backing of the photo quilt

From the batting, cut:
- One rectangle to fit the cover of the open album (See Step 1)
- One 7¼" x 9⅜" rectangle for the photo quilt

INSTRUCTIONS

1. To cover the album, open it and lay it flat on your work surface. Measure the width and height. Cut a piece of batting to this measurement. Cut the fabric using the same measurement plus 2" for all sides.

2. Glue the batting to the outside of the album.

3. Press a ¼" hem on one long side of each 2½" strip. Center and glue one strip along each side of the binder hardware with the folded edge against the metal.

4. Place the cover fabric from Step 1 on your work surface, wrong-side up. Fold the corners of the fabric diagonally over the corners of the album; glue in place.

5. Fold the short edges over the side edges of the album; glue in place.

6. Fold the long edges of the fabric over the top and bottom edges of the album, trimming the fabric to fit around the binder hardware.

7. Apply fray preventative to the trimmed edges; let dry.

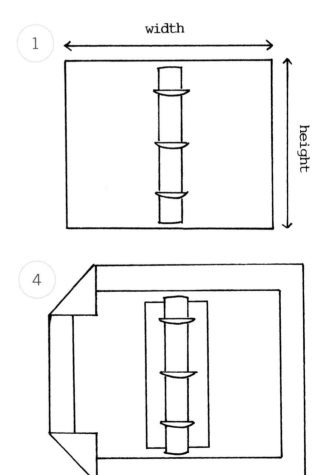

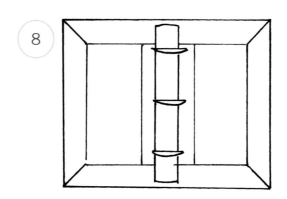

8. Glue the long edges in place, mitering the corners.

9. To cover the inside of the album, cut two pieces of cardboard ½" smaller on all sides than the front and back of the album. *Note:* The front and back measurements may differ depending on where the binder hardware is located.

10. Cut two fabric pieces 1" larger on all sides than the cardboard pieces.

11. Center the cardboard for the front inside cover on the wrong side of the appropriate fabric piece. Fold the edges of the fabric over the edges of the cardboard and glue in place. Repeat to cover the back cardboard piece with the remaining fabric.

12. Center and glue the covered cardboard pieces inside the front and back of the album.

13. Follow the manufacturer's instructions to transfer your photo onto the inkjet-printable sheet. Let dry as directed.

14. Trim the inkjet-printable fabric with the photo centered to measure 6¼" x 4⅜".

15. Sew the 4⅜" blue strips to the sides of the photo; press the seams outward.

16. Sew the 7¼" blue strips to the top and bottom of the photo; press the seams outward.

17. Sew the 7¼" plaid strips to the top and bottom of the bordered photo; press the seams outward.

18. Place the photo block and backing right sides together; pin them to the batting. Sew all around, leaving a 4" opening along the bottom.

19. Trim the batting close to the seam allowance and clip the corners. Turn the piece right-side out.

20. Fold in the seam allowance on the opening and hand sew the opening closed. Press the block well.

21. Machine quilt the block by sewing between each border, right beside the seam.

22. Center and sew three buttons to the top border and three buttons to the bottom border.

23. Glue the photo quilt to the front cover, 1½" down from the top, applying dots of glue to the back where the buttons are attached.

24. Apply fray preventative to the ends of the cord; let dry.

25. Tie a knot at each end of the cord.

26. Arrange the cord over the album front, forming loops and swirls around three sides of the photo quilt. When you are satisfied with the placement, lift a portion of the cord at a time and glue it down.

27. Paint the sheriff badge cutout with metallic gold paint; let dry.

28. Glue the badge over the cord below the photo.

"Sugar and Spice" Album

▭ 8⅜" x 13⅜"
⏱ An evening

MATERIALS

Fabric:
- ⅔ yd. pink-and-black dot print
- Scrap of dark pink print
- Fat eighth or ¼ yd. black-and-gray stripe

3-ring photo album, 8⅜" x 13⅜"
Inkjet-printable fabric sheet
6" x 4" color photo
Batting
¼ yd. pink-and-black striped ribbon, ⅞" wide
White-and-black dot fabric flower, 2¾" diameter
Round pink shank button, ⅜" diameter
18" length of black plastic-coated wire, 18-gauge
Alphabet beads, ⅛" diameter
5 pink plastic pony beads, 6mm x 9mm

Buttons:
- 4 black, 1⅛" diameter
- 4 pink, ¾" diameter

Black embroidery floss
Matching sewing threads
Permanent fabric adhesive
Scanner with inkjet color printer
Wire cutters
Needle nose pliers

CUTTING INSTRUCTIONS

From the pink-and-black dot print, cut:
- One rectangle large enough for the cover (See Step 1 in Boys' Album)
- Two rectangles large enough for the inside cover (See Step 9 in Boys' Album)
- Two 2½" x 12⅜" strips for the inside
- One 7¼" x 9⅝" rectangle for the photo quilt backing

From the dark pink print, cut:
- Two 1" x 4⅜" strips for the side borders of the photo quilt

- Two 1" x 7¼" strips for the top and bottom borders of the photo quilt

From the black stripe, cut:
- One 1¼" x 7¼" strip for the top border of the photo quilt
- One 4" x 7¼" strip for the bottom border of the photo quilt

From the batting, cut:
- One rectangle to fit the cover of the open album (See Step 1 of Boys' Album)
- One 7¼" x 9⅝" rectangle for the backing of the photo quilt

Instructions

1. Cover the photo album with the pink and black dot fabric, following the instructions for the boys' version, Steps 1 through 12.

2. Follow the manufacturer's instructions to transfer your photo onto the inkjet-printable fabric sheet. Let dry as directed.

3. Trim the inkjet-printable fabric with the photo centered to measure 6¼" x 4⅜".

4. Sew the 4⅜" dark pink strips to the sides of the photo; press the seams outward.

5. Sew the 7¼" dark pink strips to the top and bottom of the photo; press the seams outward.

6. Sew the 1¼" black strip to the top of the bordered photo; press the seam outward.

7. Sew the 4" black strip to the bottom of the bordered photo; press the seam outward.

8. Place the photo block and backing right sides together; pin them to the batting. Sew all around, leaving a 4" opening along the bottom.

9. Trim the batting close to the seam allowances and clip the corners. Turn the piece right-side out.

10. Fold in the seam allowance on the opening and hand sew the opening closed. Press the block well.

11. Machine quilt by sewing between each border, right beside the seam.

12. Glue the ribbon across the center of the bottom black border, wrapping the ends around to the back of the photo quilt.

13. Use wire cutters to remove the shank from the pink button if necessary and glue the button to the center of the flower. Glue the flower to the center of the ribbon.

14. To curl one end of the wire, hold the tip of the wire with the needle nose pliers and begin to turn the pliers, forming a small circle. Continue to bend the wire around in concentric circles, using about 7" of the wire.

15. Thread the beads onto the wire with a pony bead at each end, and three in the center between the beads spelling out "girl power" (or whatever phrase you prefer).

16. Curl the remaining end of wire in the same manner as before. Bend the center wire into a curve as shown.

17. Carefully apply glue to the back of the beads and press the piece to the bottom panel of the photo quilt with the words curving above the flower.

18. Stack one pink button on top of a black button, matching the holes. Use the floss to sew the two buttons together and glue them to one corner of the album front. Stack the remaining buttons and glue a pair to each of the other corners.

19. Glue the photo quilt to the front album cover, about 1¾" down from the top.

Tip

If you can't find a fabric flower you like, look for fabric flower pins or ponytail holders. Simply remove the pin backing or cord and the flower is ready for your project!

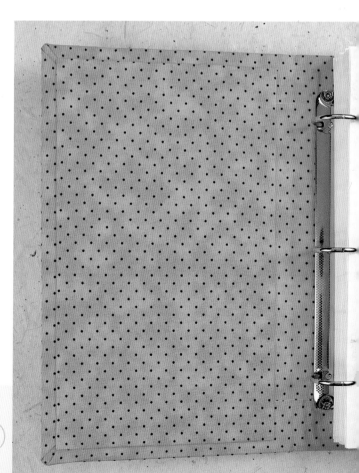

Fabric-Covered Frame

Transform a plain wooden frame with patchwork fabric, Battenberg and crocheted trims and pearl buttons. Many vintage-looking trims are available; I chose these simple pieces to adorn a copy of an old photo of my relatives.

🔲 8" x 8"
🕐 2 hours

MATERIALS

Fabric:
- Scraps of 6-8 assorted white and ivory prints for the patchwork front
- 9" x 9" piece of white or ivory print for the back

8" x 8" wood frame with flat, wide sides and a 3" x 3" opening

8" x 8" piece of batting

10" length of white flat trim, ¼" wide

White Battenberg leaf trim, 5" across

Tan crocheted flower, 2½" diameter

White shank button, ⅝" diameter

5 ivory buttons, ⅝" diameter

8" x 8" piece of lightweight cardboard

Matching sewing thread

Permanent fabric adhesive

Fray preventative

CUTTING INSTRUCTIONS

From the assorted white and ivory prints, cut:
- 36 (2½") squares

Instructions

1. Arrange the assorted white and ivory fabric squares into six rows of six squares each.

2. When you are satisfied with the combination, sew the squares in each row together. Press the seam allowances open.

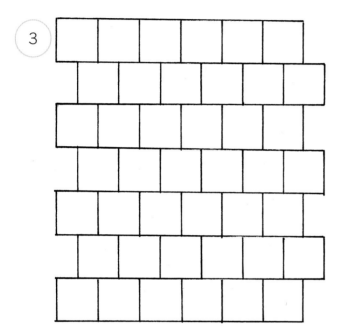

3. Before sewing the rows together, move the second, fourth and bottom row 1" to the right, so the rows are staggered. Pin the rows in this arrangement and sew the rows together.

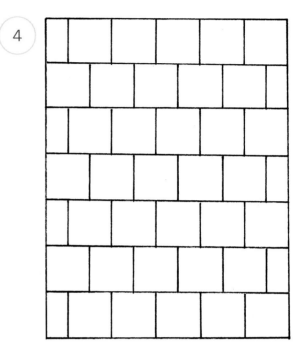

4. Trim the excess inch from each side so the completed piece is 10½" x 12½".

5. Using the frame as a pattern, cut out the center opening (for the photo) in the batting and the cardboard backing.

6. Glue the batting to the front of the frame.

7. Place the patchwork fabric right-side down on your work surface and center the frame, batting-side down, on the fabric. Holding the fabric to the frame, pick it up and see if the patchwork is arranged the way you want it. You can move the frame around a little, but be sure to leave enough fabric to cover the edges of the frame and be glued to the back.

8. When you are satisfied with the placement, mark the inner corners of the photo opening with pins or a light pencil mark. Remove the frame.

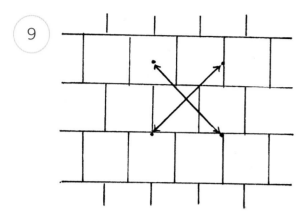

9. Cut an "X" from the inner corner marks, corner to corner. Apply fray preventative to the corners; let dry.

10. Trim the excess fabric from the opening, leaving enough to cover the inside edges and ¼" to pull to the back of the opening.

11. Lay the frame back on the fabric in the same placement. Fold and glue the fabric edges to the back of the frame along the photo opening.

12. To glue the outer frame edges, start at the midpoint of one side and pull the fabric evenly and gently to the back of the frame and glue. Repeat on the opposite side. When the sides are pulled back, finger pleat the corners and pull them to the back of the frame and glue. If necessary, trim some of the excess fabric at the corners to make them neat and flat.

13. Apply fray preventative to one end of the flat trim; let dry.

14. Starting at the lower right corner, glue the trim to the inside edge of the photo opening. Trim the end to fit and apply fray preventative. Butt the ends together and glue.

15. To cover the cardboard backing, place the cardboard on the wrong side of the fabric square. Cut an "X" for the photo opening, as in Step 9, and trim the excess fabric. Pull the fabric to the back of the cardboard and glue in place on the opening and along each side.

16. Glue the covered cardboard to the back of the frame.

17. Glue the Battenberg leaf trim to the lower right corner of the covered frame.

18. Glue the white shank button to the center of the crocheted flower.

19. Glue the flower on the leaf.

20. Glue the ivory buttons to the upper left corner of the photo opening, as shown in the photo.

What child wouldn't like to see his or her picture in a cute holiday ornament? This project also uses the photo transfer method with fabric borders sewn around the picture. The tree shape is cut from the fabric, stuffed and decorated with star buttons. The ornament shown uses a spool holder to stand upright, but you could make a hanging ornament, too.

▭ About 9" high
⏱ 1½ hours

You could make one tree for each child, making the trees taller for the older children. Or consider making a tree each year with a new picture. Be sure to write or embroider the year on the back for a wonderful remembrance.

MATERIALS

Fabric:
- Fat eighth of green print

Inkjet-printable fabric sheet

Small color photo of child (school photo size)

Polyester stuffing

Gold star button, 1" diameter

3 red star buttons, ¾" diameter

18" length of red wire-edged ribbon, ⅝" wide

Matching sewing threads

1¼" x 1⅞" wood spool with a ¼" hole

5" piece of wood dowel, ¼" diameter

Acrylic paints:
- Brown
- Gold

Small paintbrush

Scanner and color inkjet printer

Permanent fabric adhesive

Pattern:
- Tree on page 122

CUTTING INSTRUCTIONS

From the green print fabric, cut:
- Two 2½" squares
- Two 2½" x 6¼" strips

Instructions

1. Paint the wood dowel brown and the wood spool gold. Let the paint dry and set them aside.

2. Follow the manufacturer's instructions to transfer your photo onto the inkjet-printable fabric sheet. Let dry as directed.

3. Trim the fabric-printed photo to 2¼" x 2½".

4. Sew the 2½" green fabric pieces to the sides of the fabric-printed photo; press the seams outward.

5. Sew the 6¼" strips to the top and bottom of the fabric-printed photo; press the seams outward.

6. Use the pattern to cut a tree shape from the bordered photo fabric, with the bottom of the photo about 1" from the bottom of the pattern.

7. Cut a second tree from the remaining green fabric for the back of the ornament.

8. Sew the tree front and back together, right sides together, leaving a 2" opening at the bottom. Clip the curves and turn the tree right-side out.

9. Stuff the tree firmly with the polyester stuffing. Before you finish stuffing the bottom, insert one end of the dowel up into the tree about 1½". Finish pushing the stuffing up and around the dowel until it is tight.

10. Fold in the seam allowance on the opening; slip stitch the edges together on both sides of the dowel.

11. Sew the gold star button to the front top of the tree.

12. Sew the three red star buttons around the photo.

13. Insert a little glue into the hole in the spool and push the bottom end of the dowel in all the way to the other end.

14. Wrap the ribbon around the dowel at the base of the tree and tie the ends in a bow. Tie a knot at the middle and at the end of each streamer.

This purchased frame is really dressed up with a few quick and simple embellishments. I used pastel yo-yo flowers and a mini fence on a white frame for this snapshot of my mother and aunt in a garden setting. Any color combination would work — just coordinate the fabrics to the photo and your room décor.

▭ 6" x 6" frame
⏱ 1 hour

MATERIALS

Fabric:
- Scraps of 4 assorted pastel prints

6" x 6" white frame with flat sides

3 white buttons, 9/16" diameter

1 white button, 3/8" diameter

10" length of green satin ribbon, 7/8" wide

1½" x 2¼" piece of white picket fence (found in craft supply stores)

Matching sewing threads

Permanent fabric adhesive

Patterns:
- Large Yo-Yo Flower on page 122
- Small Yo-Yo Flower on page 122

Instructions

1. Use the patterns to cut three large and one small circle from the assorted pastel prints.

2. Refer to the Yo-Yo Embellishments instructions on page 19 to make the flowers from the fabric circles.

3. Sew a ⁹⁄₁₆"-diameter white button to the center of each large yo-yo flower with thread to match the fabric. Sew the ³⁄₈" button to the small yo-yo flower.

4. Cut the satin ribbon into five 2" lengths.

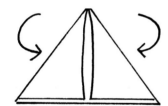

5. To make a leaf from each piece of ribbon, find the center on one long side and finger press it. Fold each top corner down to match the bottom edge at the center.

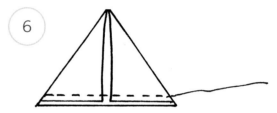

6. Hand sew gathering stitches ⅛" from the bottom edge. Pull the thread to gather the bottom and form the leaf.

7. Wrap the thread around the bottom; knot and clip the thread. Repeat Steps 5-7 to make a total of five leaves.

8. Glue the fence section to the bottom left corner at a slight angle.

9. Glue two large and one small flower to the fence and one large flower to the upper right corner. Apply the glue to just the center back of the flowers so the edges are free.

10. Glue leaves around the flowers by lifting the edge of the flower and tucking the end of the leaf underneath to cover the raw edges.

Sew Much Fun

This chapter focuses on an activity we all love — sewing! These projects have form, function and a cheerful appeal with an assortment of bright polka dot fabrics. The soft, freeform rag rope basket is garnished with a colorful fabric band and yo-yo flower. The bulletin board organizer starts with a patchwork shape that folds up to make a pocket for supplies. The scissors holder and mug pincushion are made from the same coordinating fabrics.

Rag Rope Basket

Made from soft piping cord and fabric strips, this basket is easy to make and rather addictive — you will want one near all your favorite chairs to hold hand sewing projects, knitting, or even a plant. The cord is completely wrapped with fabric strips and wound into a basket form, with an extra wrap every few inches to hold the shape.

▥ Approximately 9½" x 8" x 5" high
⏱ An evening

You can make any size or rounded shape basket you would like just by following the same simple steps. You could also use an assortment of fabrics for a more colorful, scrappy look, or to make different colored stripes on the basket.

MATERIALS

Fabric:
- ⅔ yd. black-and-white dotted print
- ⅛ yd. yellow dotted print
- Scrap of red dotted prints
- Scrap of green dotted prints

9 yd. cotton piping filler, ½" diameter

Black button, ¾" diameter

Matching sewing threads

Transparent or masking tape

Permanent fabric adhesive

Patterns:
- Yo-Yo Flower on page 123
- Leaf on page 123

CUTTING INSTRUCTIONS

From the black-and-white dotted print, cut:
- 32 (¾" x 45") strips

Instructions

1. Starting at one end of the piping, anchor one end of a fabric strip with a dot of glue and wrap the strip around the cord in a spiral fashion.

2. With each wrap, overlap the previous strip about ¼". When you have 4" of the cord covered, fold the cord back on itself about 2½" from the end. Wrap the fabric once over both cords.

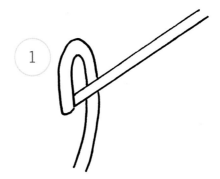

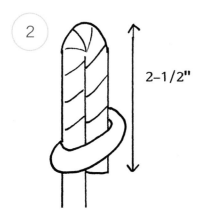

2

2-1/2"

3. Continue to wrap the cord with the fabric. As you wrap, coil the cord into an oval shape. Stabilize the shape every few inches by wrapping the strip over the adjacent covered cord. The rows push apart easily to make this extra wrap.

4. When a strip runs out, use a dot of glue to adhere the end to the cord. Start the new strip by overlapping the ends slightly and use a dot of glue to hold it. Place the overlapped end on a place on the cord that will be covered by the next row. Continue enlarging the oval base until it measures about 7" x 6".

5. Start coiling the cord on top of the base at the outer edge and begin to build up the sides. Every few inches, wrap the fabric strip once over the row below to stabilize the shape.

6. When the basket is about 3½" high, form the brim by making the next three rows just slightly wider. The basket should be about 5" tall at this point.

7. When you are ready to finish, wrap a small piece of tape around the place on the cord where you want to cut. Wrap the rope up to a few inches from the tape and cut through the center of the taped cord.

8. To cover the end, cut a 1" piece from a fabric strip and glue it to the end. Finish wrapping the cord and end with a strip that goes through the row below. Secure the end with a dot of glue.

9. For the fabric band, measure loosely around the basket, about 3 rows down. Add 1" to this measurement. Cut a strip from the yellow dotted print the length of this measurement and 2½" wide.

10. Fold the strip in half lengthwise right sides together, and sew the long edges together. Turn it right-side out and press.

11. Wrap the fabric strip around the basket and overlap the end at the center front. Glue the ends together.

12. Use the pattern to cut a circle from the red dotted fabric. Follow the Yo-Yo Embellishment instructions on page 19 to make the flower.

13. Sew the black button in the center of the flower.

14. Apply glue to the back of the flower, just in the center, and press it to the band front, covering the overlapped ends.

15. Use the pattern to draw the leaf two times on the wrong side of the green dotted print.

16. Fold the fabric in half, right sides together, with the two patterns on top. Sew on the traced lines, leaving an opening at the bottom.

17. Cut the leaves out ⅛" from the seam and turn right-side out.

18. Pinch a pleat at the wide end of each leaf and use a dot of glue to hold it.

19. Apply glue and tuck a leaf under the edge of the flower on each side.

This padded scissors holder protects the scissors from nicks and the user from unexpected jabs. Fusible fleece makes it sturdy and the binding all around is functional and decorative. I made it large enough to hold two or three pairs of scissors.

4⅞" x 9"

1½ hours

If you do a lot of hand sewing and like to keep your small scissors close at hand, reduce the pattern size and make a chatelaine. Attach a ribbon end to each side and wear it around your neck while you sew. The padded fabric can hold your needle and pins.

MATERIALS

Fabric:
- Fat quarter of black dotted print
- Fat quarter of green dotted print

10" x 10" piece of fusible fleece

Matching sewing threads

Patterns:
- Scissors Holder Back on page 124
- Scissors Holder Front on page 125

Instructions

1. Follow the manufacturer's instructions to fuse the fleece to the wrong side of a section of the black dotted fabric.

2. Use the patterns to cut one back and one front from the fused fabric and one back and one front from a section of the fabric that does not have fleece for the lining.

3. Pin the two front pieces right sides together at the top; sew the top. Clip along the curve. Flip the lining over, sandwiching the fleece between the two layers. Press the seam.

4. Layer the two back pieces so that the fleece is in the middle and the right sides of the fabric are facing out. Baste the raw edges together all around.

5. Pin the scissors holder front and back pieces together, matching the lower edge and sides. Machine baste the layers together ³⁄₁₆" from the edge.

6. Cut a 2¼" x 24" binding strip from the bias of the green dotted fabric. Use your ruler to find the 45-degree angle on the fabric and cut on this diagonal line. Move the ruler and cut again to make a 2¼"-wide strip.

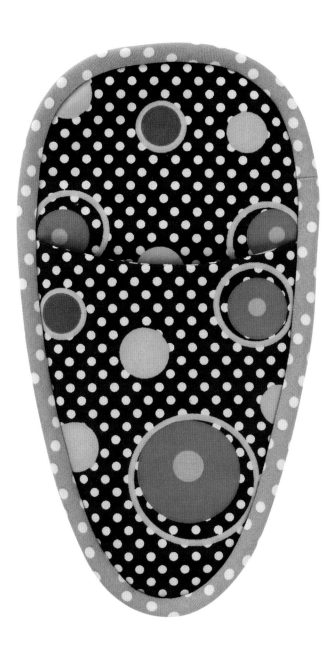

7. Fold the strip in half lengthwise, wrong sides together, and press, being careful not to stretch the fabric.

8. Place the binding strip on top of the holder on one side, matching the raw edges. Starting 2" from the end of the strip, sew around with a ¼" seam allowance. When you are near the beginning point, stop sewing. Overlap the binding ½" from the edge and trim away any excess.

9. Pick up the two ends and join them in a ¼" seam; press the seam open. Reposition the joined binding along the edge of the holder and resume stitching to the beginning.

10. Bring the folded edge of the binding strip over to the back of the scissors holder (*Note:* The back of the binding is wider than the front). Sew on the front side, right next to the binding seam, so the stitches will catch the binding on the back.

Tip

Using black thread on the top and green in the bobbin will make the stitches blend into the fabric.

Bulletin Board Organizer

Sew squares of polka dot fabrics to make the top portion of this handy organizer. The bottom section folds up to form a pocket perfect for all of your sewing inspirations. Glue buttons to thumbtacks for unique push pins on the bulletin board. The organizer can also be used over the arm of a chair to hold tools and patterns.

8" x 15"

2 hours

MATERIALS

Fabric:
- ¼ yd. black print with dots
- Scraps of 4-8 assorted dotted prints
- ⅛ yd. yellow dotted print

8" x 20½" piece of batting

2 plastic rings, 1" diameter, for hangers

Assorted small buttons

Thumbtacks

Matching sewing threads

Metal glue

CUTTING INSTRUCTIONS

From the black dotted print, cut:
- Four 3" squares for patchwork
- One 8" x 10½" rectangle for the pocket
- One 8" x 20½" rectangle for the backing

From the assorted dotted prints, cut:
- Eight 3" squares for patchwork

From the yellow dotted print, cut:
- One 2¼" x 44" strip for the binding

Instructions

1. Arrange the 3" squares into four rows of three squares each.

2. Sew the squares in each row together. Press the seam allowances in one direction, alternating the direction for each row.

3. Sew the rows together to make an 8" x 10½" rectangle.

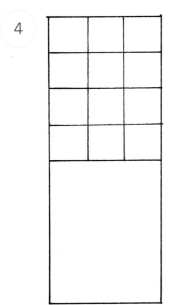

4. Sew the black 8" x 10½" rectangle to the bottom of the patchwork. The piece should now measure 8" x 20½".

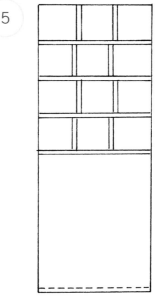

5. Hold the backing and the pieced top right sides together, and place the layers on top of the batting. Sew a seam along the short, unpieced end.

6. Trim the batting close to the seam and flip the top layer over so the batting is now sandwiched between the front and back layer. Press the seam.

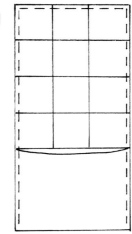

7. Fold up the seamed end 5" to form a pocket. The piece should now measure 8" x 15". Machine or hand baste all the raw edges together about ³⁄₁₆" from the edge.

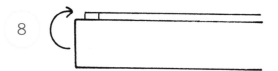

8. Fold and press a ½" hem at one short end of the binding strip. Fold the strip in half lengthwise, wrong sides together, and press.

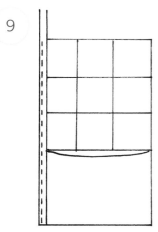

9. Starting at the lower left corner of the organizer, place the hemmed end of the binding on top of the organizer. Sew through all layers with a ¼" seam up to the top corner. Stop sewing ¼" from the corner, backstitch, and then clip the threads. Remove the piece from the sewing machine.

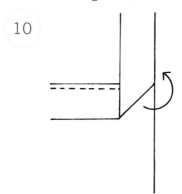

10. Fold the binding upward, creating a 45-degree diagonal fold, and finger press.

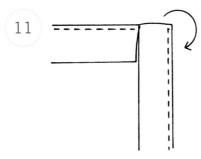

11. Fold the binding back down, matching the raw edges and aligning the top fold with the top of the organizer. Begin sewing again at the edge of the corner.

12. Sew across the top and stop ¼" away from the other corner. Follow Steps 9-11 to miter the corner, and continue sewing down the other side. Before you reach the bottom, trim off the excess binding and fold in a ½" hem.

13. To finish, bring the folded edge of the binding over the raw edges to the back. Hand stitch the binding to the backing fabric.

14. To finish the corners on the back, stitch up to a corner and fold the binding strip into a miter and secure with a few small stitches.

15. Slipstitch the folded ends of the binding together at the bottom, to close in all the raw edges.

16. Hand sew a plastic ring to each top corner on the back of the organizer for hangers. *Note:* If you want use the organizer on the arm of your chair, anchor it with safety pins.

17. To make a button tack, glue a button to the top of a thumbtack. Let the glue set before using the tack.

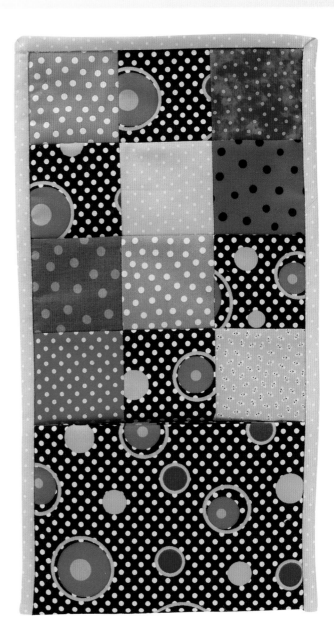

Coffee Mug Pincushion

You won't have any trouble finding this pincushion — it's as decorative as it is functional. The pincushion top is a circle of fabric over stuffing and the strawberry emery hangs down ready to sharpen your needles and pins.

⬛ 6" high

🕐 1 hour

Strawberry emeries have been a staple in our sewing baskets for years. Sharpen pins and needles by sliding them in and out of the emery. Bulk emery is no longer available; the commercial emeries are filled with silicon carbide or sterilized sand. I took apart an old emery to fill my new strawberry. If you prefer, you can pull apart wool batting and use it to fill the strawberry. It won't sharpen the pins and needles, but the lanolin from the wool will help prevent them from rusting.

MATERIALS

Fabric:
- Fat quarter of black dotted print
- Scraps of red print, muslin and green felt

Coffee mug, about 3" across at the top

10" length of green grosgrain ribbon, ⅜" wide

Polyester stuffing

Silicon carbide or wool batting (see Emery sidebar above)

Dinner plate (for pattern)

Heavy-duty thread

Paper envelope

Permanent fabric adhesive

Patterns:
- Strawberry on page 123
- Strawberry Top on page 123

MUG

1. Cut an 11" circle from the black dotted print. An average dinner plate is a good source for a pattern.

2. Use a doubled length of heavy-duty thread to hand sew gathering stitches around the edge of the fabric circle. Place a ball of stuffing in the middle of the fabric, on the wrong side, and start to pull the thread to gather the fabric edges and form a ball. Keep adding stuffing until the ball is fairly firm. Knot and clip the thread.

3. Place the fabric ball on top of the mug and start to tuck the sides into the mug. It should fit snugly and extend above the rim a few inches.

STRAWBERRY

1. Use the pattern to cut one strawberry each from the red print and the muslin. Cut one strawberry top from the green felt.

2. Fold the muslin in half, forming a quarter circle, and sew a ⅛" seam down the straight edges. Trim the tip and turn the strawberry right-side out.

3. Use a double strand of heavy thread to hand sew gathering stitches around the top edge of the strawberry.

4. Fill the muslin strawberry liner with silicon carbide, using an envelope with a corner cut off as a funnel. Or pull wool batting apart and stuff the strawberry with it.

5. Pull the thread to gather the top edges together; knot and clip the thread.

6. Fold the red print strawberry in half, right sides together, and sew the straight edges with a ⅛" seam. Trim the tip and turn it right-side out.

7. Hand gather around the top edge.

8. Insert the filled muslin liner. Draw the gathers up over the top of the muslin emery. Knot and clip the thread.

9. Cut a 2½" length of ribbon. Cut a short slash in the center of the felt strawberry top; slip one end of this ribbon through the slash and glue it to the other side. Glue the felt top to the top of the strawberry with the longer end of the ribbon extending up.

10. Decide where you would like to attach the strawberry emery and gently push the pincushion ball away from the mug. Apply glue to the end of the ribbon and tuck it inside, between the pincushion and the mug.

11. Tie the remaining ribbon in a bow; glue it to the top of the ribbon hanger.

Bon Voyage

"Bon voyage" means "good journey," and this set of projects is designed to enhance any travel plans. The roomy tote bag and coordinating embellished wool hat are practical accessories for the traveler. The map holder has handy pockets for maps and notes and folds into a compact size for packing. The purchased photo box holds remnants of your travels and can be a part of the room décor.

This attractive tote bag is sturdy and practical with a navy check exterior and a bright red-and-white polka dot lining. The ready-made flower trim has been embellished with a polka dot center and leaves.

▭ 14" x 11" x 3"
⏱ An evening

MATERIALS

Fabric:
- ¾ yd. navy blue check, home dec. weight
- ½ yd. red-and-white dot
- Scraps of green and yellow dot

¾ yd. fusible fleece

Scrap of plain fleece

2 navy blue buttons, 1¼" diameter

Shank button, 1¼" diameter

4½" purchased fabric flower

2⅞" x 14" piece of plastic needlepoint canvas or cardboard for the bottom of the tote

Pin back (optional)

Matching sewing threads

Permanent fabric adhesive

Patterns:
- Leaf on page 126
- Flower Center on page 126

CUTTING INSTRUCTIONS

From the navy blue check, cut:
- Two 14½" x 11½" rectangles for the front and back
- One 3½" x 37½" strip for the gusset
- Two 3" x 24" strips for the handles
- One 9" x 9" square for the pocket

From the red-and-white dot, cut:
- Two 14½" x 11½" rectangles
- One 3½" x 37½" strip
- One 9" x 9" square

From the fusible fleece, cut:
- Two 14½" x 11½" rectangles
- One 3½" x 37½" strip

Instructions

1. Follow the manufacturer's instructions to bond the matching fusible fleece pieces to the wrong side of the tote front rectangle, tote back rectangle and the gusset strip. Work from the center of each piece to the outside edges.

2. To make the pocket, sew the two 9" pocket squares right sides together, leaving one side open. Trim the corners and turn the pocket right-side out. Press well.

3. Baste the bottom edges of the pocket together.

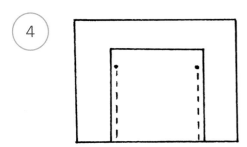

4. Center and pin the pocket on the right side of the tote front, with the raw edges of the pocket at the bottom edge of the tote. Topstitch the pocket to the tote ¼" from the edge on both sides, but stop and backstitch 1¾" from the top corners.

5. Fold the top edge of the pocket down so the lining shows; sew a navy blue button at each top corner, sewing through all the layers.

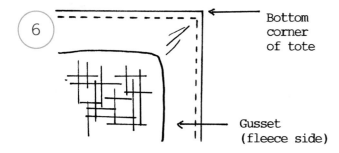

6. Pin and stitch one long edge of the fleece-stabilized gusset down one side, across the bottom and up the other side of the tote front. Trim the gusset end even with the tote front if necessary.

7. Stitch the other long edge of the gusset to the side, bottom and side of the tote back. Press both seam allowances and clip the corners. Turn the tote right-side out.

8. To make the handles, fold each of the blue check strips in half lengthwise with the right sides together. Stitch the long edge, leaving both ends open.

9. Turn the handle straps right-side out and press, bringing the seam to the center of the handle. This will be the underside of the handle.

10. Topstitch both sides of the handles ¼" from the edge.

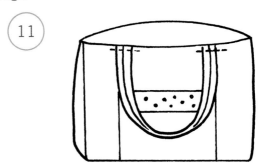

11. Pin the ends of one handle to the right side of the tote front, 2¾" from the side seams and matching the short end of the handle to the top edge of the tote. The seam on the handle should be facing out. Stitch in place.

12. Sew the remaining handle to the tote back in the same manner.

13. Sew a long edge of the gusset lining to the sides and bottom of the front lining. Sew the remaining long edge of the gusset lining to the sides and bottom of the back lining. Press the seam allowances and trim the corners. Do not turn right-side out.

Tip

Make the red dot lining in the same way as the tote.

14. Fold under a ¼" hem at the upper edge of the lining and press.

15. Place the needlepoint mesh or cardboard in the bottom of the tote.

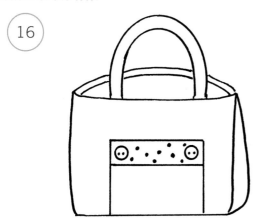

16. Fold the tote handles up and press a ¼" hem in at the top of the tote.

17. Insert the lining into the tote shell, matching the side seams.

18. Slipstitch the folded edge of the lining to the folded edge of the tote.

19. Topstitch all around the top of the tote, ¼" from the edge.

20. Trace the leaf pattern two times on the wrong side of the green dot fabric. Fold the fabric in half, with the traced pattern on top, and pin the fabric to the scrap of fleece.

21. Sew all around on the pattern lines, leaving the bottom edge open.

22. Cut the leaves out about ⅛" from the seam. Trim the fleece close to the seam.

23. Fold in the raw edges of each leaf and pinch a pleat in the center. Glue or tack the pleat in place. Glue the leaves to the back of the flower.

24. For the flower center, glue a scrap of fleece to the top of the shank button and trim the fleece to fit.

25. Use the pattern to cut a circle from the yellow dot fabric. Follow the Button Embellishments instructions on page 17 to cover the shank button. Glue or sew the center to the flower.

26. Glue the completed flower to the tote front, or attach a pin back to the flower and pin it in place.

When you create a special embellishment for a project, attach it with a pin back or a safety pin so you can use it on other items as well.

Fabric-Covered Photo Box

Turn an ordinary photo box into a whimsical accessory for your family room with fabrics and simple techniques. This one has a cork layer under the top travel-theme fabric and a push pin made from a toy car, perfect for highlighting some special pictures or souvenirs.

⟁ 7⅝" x 11" x 4¾"

⏱ 2 hours

Choose your fabrics to coordinate with your travels: Oriental fabrics for a trip to Asia, London and Paris motifs for a European trip, or cowboy figures for a trip west. A water or boat print for a cruise, Khaki and plaid for a camping trip ... you get the idea. The push pins can be personalized, too, by using small planes, boats, sea shells, or anything that reminds you of that special trip.

MATERIALS

Fabric:
- ½ yd. navy blue check, home dec. weight
- ½ yd. novelty fabric with travel theme
- ⅛ yd. red mini-check

Photo box with lid (the featured box is 7⅝" x 11" x 4¾")

White pearl cotton, size 5

Cork sheet or batting to fit top of lid

2" x 2" slide mount (found with scrapbooking supplies)

16" length taupe suede lace, ⁵⁄₃₂" wide

2 nickel pronged spots, ¼"

Scrap of white cardstock

Mini metal car

Thumbtack

Computer font or permanent black marking pen

Embroidery needle

Fray preventative

Spray adhesive

Permanent fabric adhesive

Metal adhesive

CUTTING INSTRUCTIONS

From the navy blue check, cut:
- One 6" x 38" strip
- One 7⅝" x 11" rectangle

From the novelty print, cut:
- One 13½" x 17" rectangle

From the red mini-check, cut:
- One 4½" x 40" strip
- One 3" x 3" square

Instructions

Note: Use the spray adhesive for large flat areas of gluing and the fabric adhesive for fabric ends or when using a spray would make it difficult to keep the front side of the fabric clean.

1. If a metal bookplate is attached to the box, remove it.

2. Apply fray preventative to all sides of the two blue check pieces; let dry.

3. Glue one short end of the 38" checked strip to the side of the box, starting about 1" before the corner on the back of the box. Keep an equal margin of fabric at the top and bottom and glue the strip all around the box. Overlap the ends at the back and trim any excess fabric.

4. Fold the extra fabric at the top to the inside of the box and glue in place.

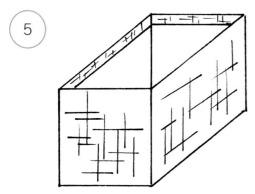

5. Fold the extra fabric at the lower edge to the bottom of the box and glue in place.

6. To finish the box, glue the blue check rectangle to the bottom.

7. If you would like to use push pins on the top of the box, measure and cut a piece of cork to fit the top of the lid. Glue the cork in place. If you are not using cork, cut a piece of batting to fit and glue it to the top of the lid.

8. Place the novelty print on your work surface, wrong-side up. Center the lid, cork or batting-side down, on the fabric.

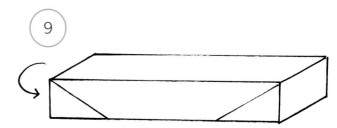

9. Working one side at a time, apply glue to the edge of the fabric and pull it up and over the side and press it to the inside edge of the lid. To fit the corners, fold the extra fabric toward the long side of the lid and glue it down.

10. Fold the red check strip in half lengthwise, right sides together, and sew one short end and the long edges together.

11. Trim the corners and turn the strip right-side out; press.

12. Sew a running stitch along all the long sides and the closed end of the strip with one strand of the pearl cotton cord.

13. Hold the finished (closed) end of the strip up to a back corner of the lid. Start to glue the strip to the sides of the lid about 2" from the finished end. When the strip is all the way around the lid, tuck the raw edge under the finished end and glue in place.

14. To cover the slide mount, center it over the red check square, with the front of the slide on the wrong side of the fabric. Pull the outside edges of the fabric to the back of the slide mount and glue them in place, trimming the excess fabric at the corners.

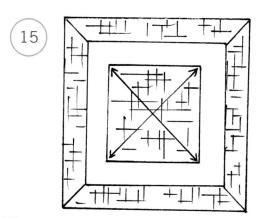

15. For the inside edges, cut an "X" in the center fabric, from corner to corner.

16. Fold the fabric to the inside of the frame and glue in place, trimming the excess fabric in the middle.

17. Using a computer font or a permanent black marking pen, print or write an appropriate label on the white cardstock.

18. Trim the cardstock to fit the slide mount frame. Glue it to the inside.

19. Cut the lacing in half and wrap each piece around a side of the frame. Wrap it twice with both ends extending out to the side.

20. Glue the slide mount label to the front of the box, under the lid, with the laces out to the side. Insert the pronged spots over the laces and flatten the prong points on the inside of the box.

21. Use the metal adhesive to glue the underside of the car to the top of the thumbtack. When the glue is set, insert the car tack into the cork on the top of the box.

These boxes usually come with dividers for the inside. If you have a little more time, these could be decorated with collage papers (copy souvenirs and itineraries), rubber stamps and personal notes.

Map Holder

This clever accessory is made from a placemat with pockets and elastic added to hold maps, notes, pencils and tour guide. When it folds up, it fits neatly in the tote or car seat pocket.

▭ 18" x 13" open and 6" x 13" closed
🕐 1½ hours

MATERIALS

Fabric:
- Fat quarter of black-and-red plaid

18" x 13" medium-body brown placemat

8½" x 11" sheet of inkjet-printable fabric

Map page or map-themed scrapbook paper

Scrap of fleece

5" piece of black elastic, ¾" wide

2 brown buttons, ¾" diameter

2 black buttons, 1⅛" diameter

1 yd. red grosgrain ribbon, ⅞" wide

Letter cutouts (leather, vinyl or felt) to spell "road trips," about ⅞" high

Black quilting or heavy-duty thread

Matching sewing threads

Fray preventative

Permanent fabric adhesive

Scanner with inkjet printer

Patterns:
- Large Map Pocket on page 127
- Small Map Pocket on page 126

Instructions

1. Follow the manufacturer's instructions to scan and print the map page onto the inkjet-printable fabric sheet, using a black and white setting; let dry.

2. Use the pattern to cut one large map pocket from the map fabric for the pocket front and one from the plaid for the lining.

3. Use the pattern to cut two small map pockets from the plaid for the front and lining.

4. Place the two large pocket pieces right sides together and pin to a layer of fleece. Do the same with the two small map pocket pieces.

5. Sew all around each pocket, leaving a 3" opening at the bottom for turning.

6. Clip the corners and trim the fleece close to the seam. Turn each pocket right-side out through the opening.

7. Fold in the seam allowance on the opening of each pocket and hand sew the opening closed.

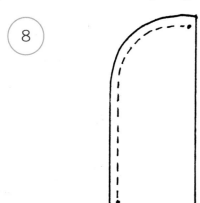

8. Topstitch the curved top and side of the small pocket, ¼" from the edge, starting and stopping ¼" from the corners.

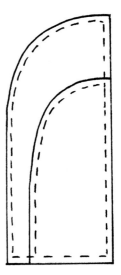

9. Place the small pocket on top of the large pocket front, matching the straight side edges and the bottom. Top stitch all around, sewing through both pockets where they overlap.

10. Apply glue to the back of the large pocket along the straight edge and bottom only. Press the pocket to the inside of the placemat with the pocket lined up with the bottom and right side edge of the placemat.

11. Apply fray preventative to the cut ends of the elastic; let dry.

12. Fold the placemat in thirds and mark the center third with pins for a guide to attach the elastic on the inside and the ribbon on the outside.

13. The buttons holding the elastic and the buttons holding the ribbon are sewn at the same points. Center the elastic on the inside of the placemat. Sew a brown button to each end of the elastic, sewing through the placemat.

14. Center the ribbon on the outside of the placemat. At the points where the inside buttons were attached, sew a black button through the ribbon, placemat and the inside button. Make several stitches back and forth through all the layers.

15. Fold the placemat back in thirds. Wrap the ribbon ends around to the front and tie them in a bow.

16. Center the letters to spell "road trips" above the bow; glue each letter in place.

This project begins with a purchased wool hat in a beautiful shade of red. The band is made from the tote's navy blue check fabric and the flower is a simple design of stitched petal circles with a button center. This project is quick and easy, but with a tailored, cosmopolitan flair.

 1 hour

All kinds of hats and all manners of flowers and trims can be combined for an embellished hat. Try a baseball cap with a sequined flower or a straw hat with flowing ribbons and silk flowers. Even a rain hat can be dressed up with waterproof vinyl cutouts.

MATERIALS

Fabric:
- ⅛ yd. blue check, home dec. weight
- Scrap of dark blue wool felt

Red wool hat

Brown leather shank button, 1" diameter

White pearl cotton thread, size 5

4½" x 4½" scrap of fusible adhesive

Embroidery needle

Permanent fabric adhesive

Patterns:
- Flower Petal on page 126

CUTTING INSTRUCTIONS

Note: The model is a "one size fits all," but you should measure your hat before cutting the band that fits around the brim. Add 2" to the measurement.

From the navy blue check, cut:
- One 1½" x (circumference + 2") strip for the band

Instructions

1. Fold the band strip in half lengthwise with right sides together and sew along the long edges. Turn the band right-side out.

2. Fold the band so the seam is centered on one side and press.

3. Wrap the band around the hat, with the seamed side next to the hat. Overlap the ends just to one side of the center front and glue the ends in place.

4. Follow the manufacturer's instructions to apply the fusible adhesive to the wrong side of the blue check fabric. Remove the paper backing and bond the fabric to the scrap of blue felt.

5. Use the pattern to cut six flower petals from this bonded fabric.

6. Sew a running stitch with one strand of white pearl cotton around the edges of each petal, about ⅛" from the edge.

7. Arrange the petals in a circle on your work surface, overlapping the edges and creating a ½" opening in the center. The flower will measure about 3" in diameter. Lift each overlapping petal to apply the glue and press in place.

8. Glue the button to the center of the flower. Clip the shank if it protrudes too far. Glue the flower to the hat band, covering the overlapped ends.

Patterns

FOR THE LOVE OF GARDENING

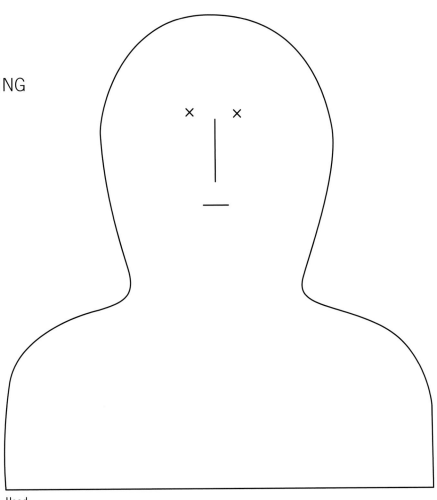

Head

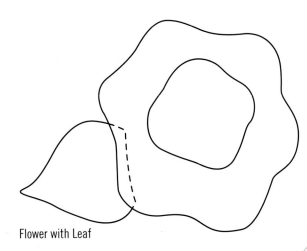

"garden journal" Embroidery Pattern

Flower with Leaf

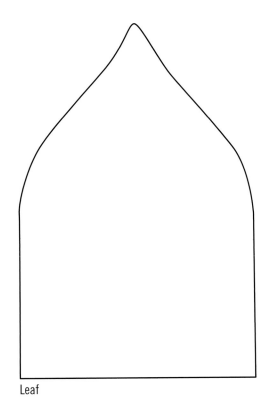

Leaf

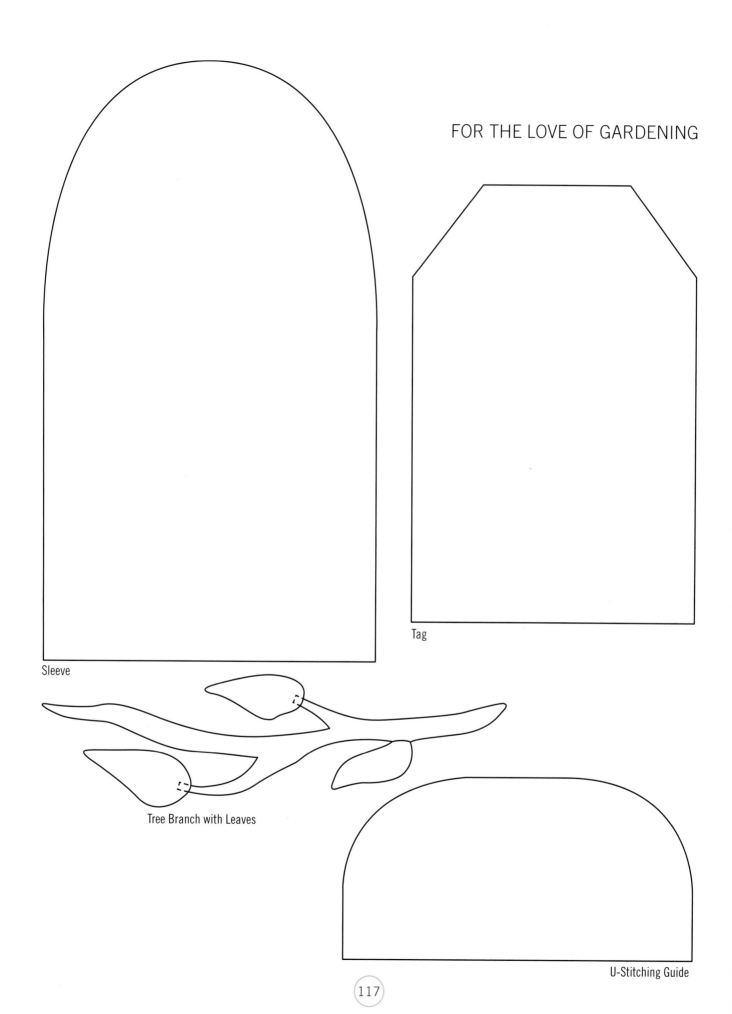

FOR THE LOVE OF GARDENING

Sleeve

Tag

Tree Branch with Leaves

U-Stitching Guide

117

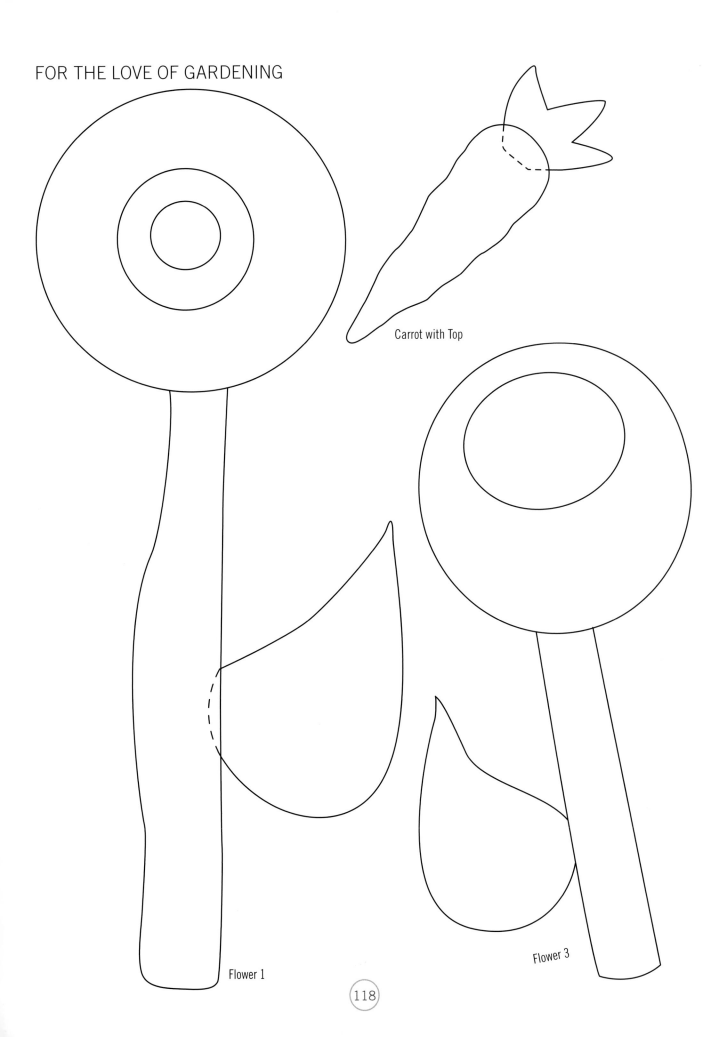

Carrot with Top

Flower 1

Flower 3

Flower Center

Flower 2

Friendship Embroidery Pattern

Heart Quilting Pattern

Fabric Insert

Heart Ornament

Small Heart Appliqué

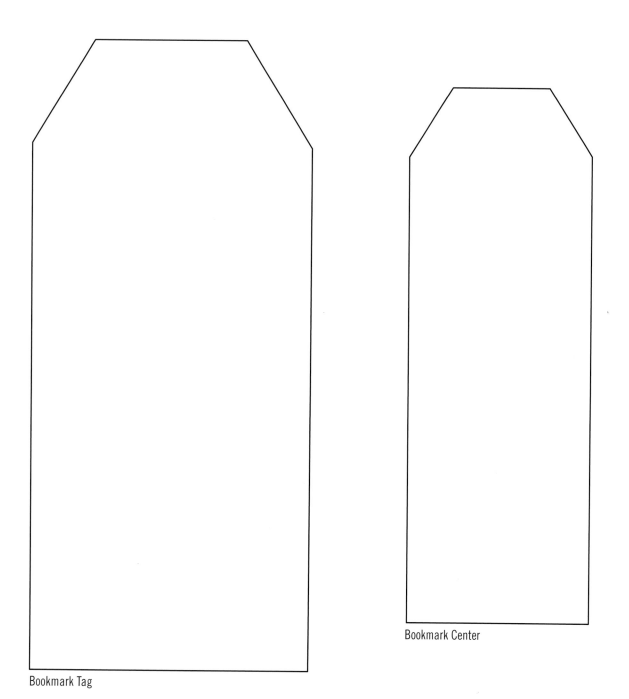

Bookmark Tag

Bookmark Center

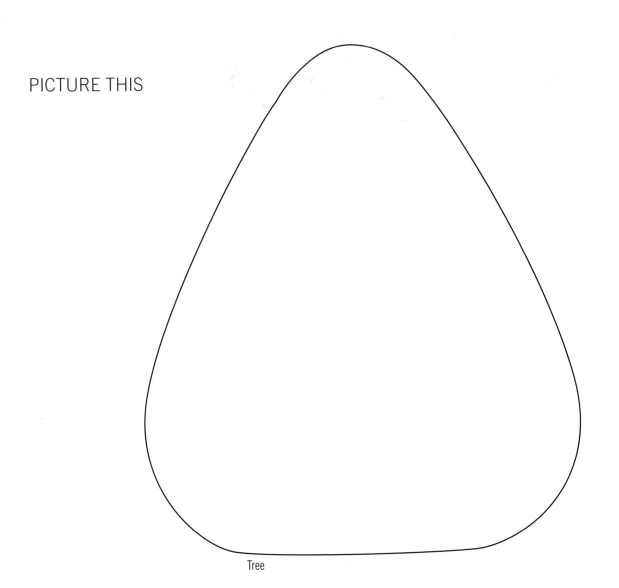

Tree

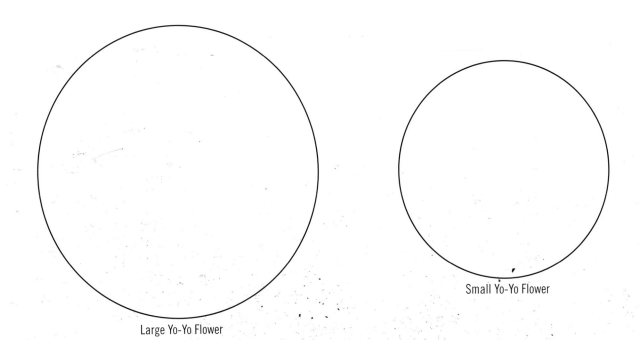

Large Yo-Yo Flower

Small Yo-Yo Flower

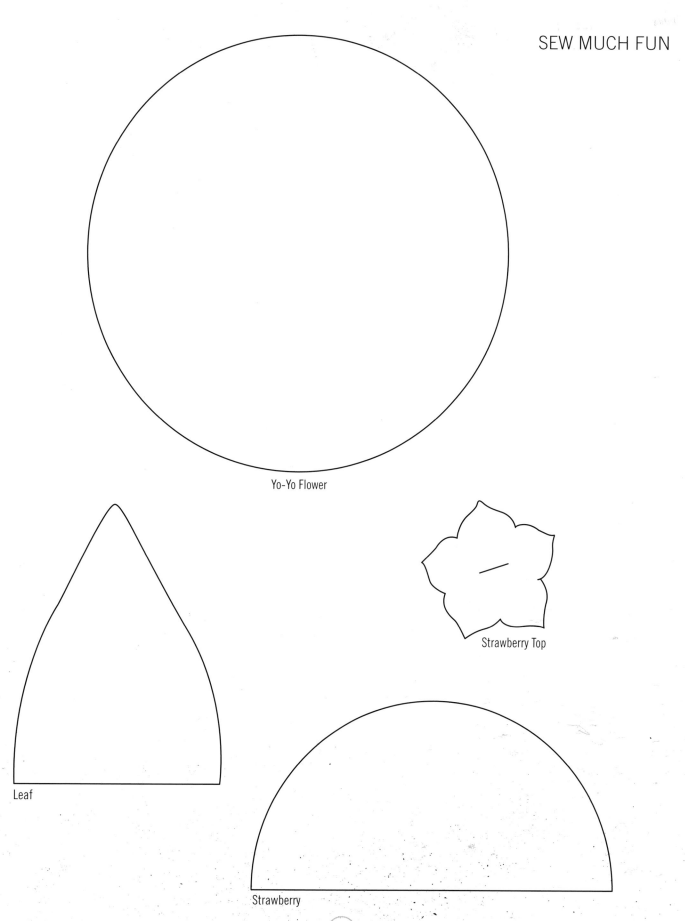

Yo-Yo Flower

Strawberry Top

Leaf

Strawberry

SEW MUCH FUN

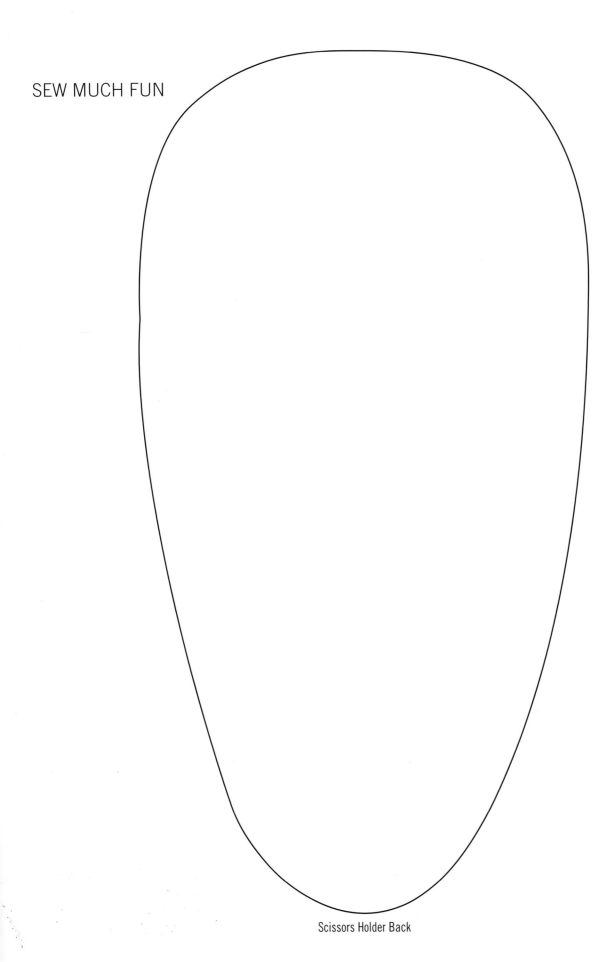

Scissors Holder Back

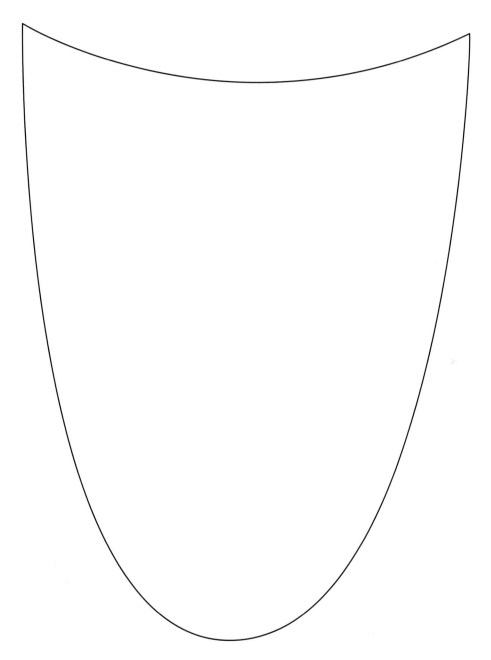

Scissors Holder Front

BON VOYAGE

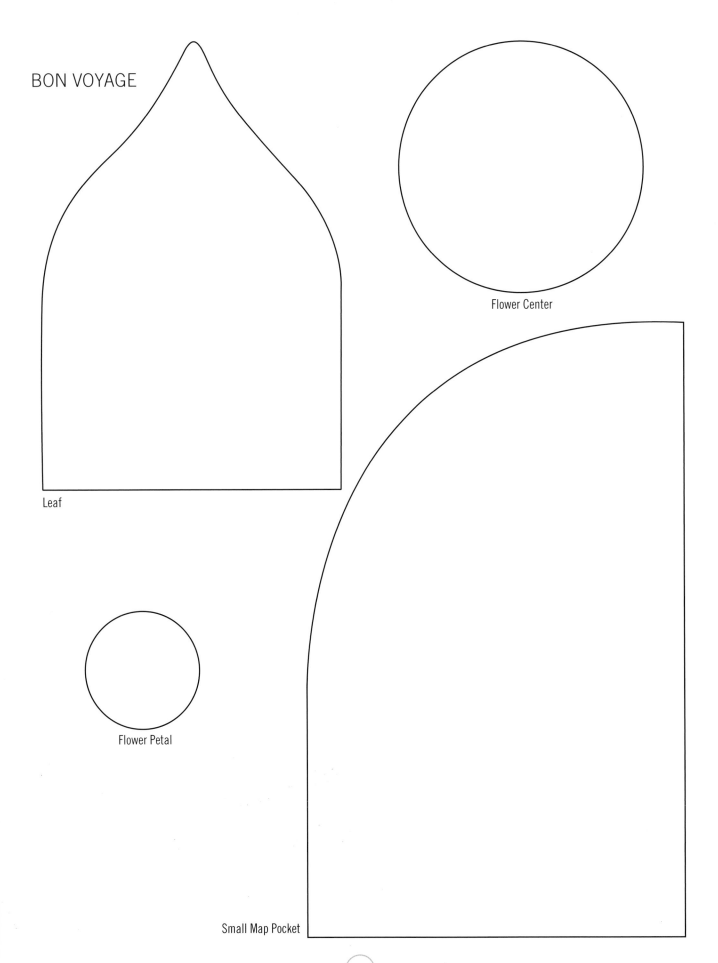

Leaf

Flower Center

Flower Petal

Small Map Pocket

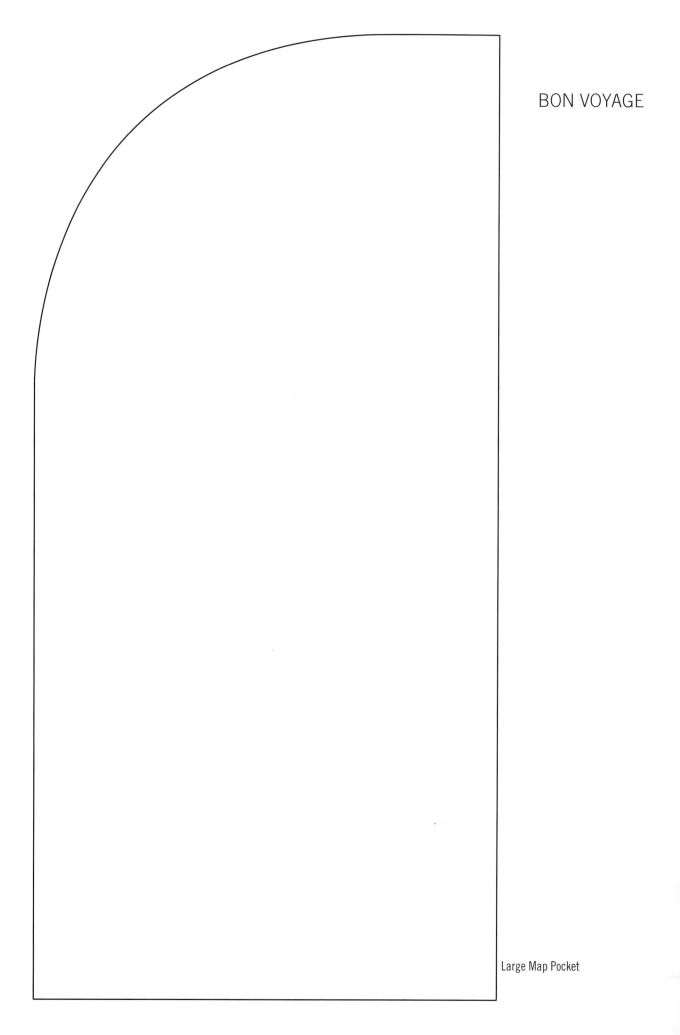

BON VOYAGE

Large Map Pocket

Resources

Beacon Adhesives, Inc.
125 MacQuesten Parkway S.
Mt. Vernon, NY 10550
(800) 865-7238
www.beaconcreates.com
Fabri-Tac™ Permanent Fabric Adhesive,
Glass, Metal & More™ Adhesive

Blumenthal Lansing Co.
One Palmer Terrace
Carlstadt, NJ 07072
(800) 448-9749
www.buttonsplus.com
Crafter's Images™ Photo Fabric™

Clotilde®
P.O. Box 7500
Big Sandy, TX 75755-7500
www.clotilde.com
Notions, tools, organizers

DMC® Corp.
S. Hackensack Avenue
Port Kearny Building #10-F
South Kearney, NJ 07032
www.dmc-usa.com
Embroidery floss, pearl cotton, quilting
thread

Fiskars® Brands, Inc.
7811 W. Stewart Ave.
Wausau, WI 54401
(715) 842-2091
www.fiskars.com
Scissors, rotary cutting systems

Freudenberg Nonwovens
3440 Industrial Drive
Durham, NC 27704
Pellon® Fusible Fleece

Hampton Art Stamps
19 Industrial Boulevard
Medford, NY 11763
(631) 924-1335
www.hamptonart.com
DF 2204 "A Friend" rubber stamp

Hansen's Brand Source
990 W. Fulton St.
Waupaca, WI 54981
(715) 258-7803
www.homeappliances.com/hansen

Krause Publications
(888) 457-2873
www.krause.com

Nancy's Notions
333 Beichl Avenue
Beaver Dam, WI 53916-0683
(800) 833-0690
www.nancysnotions.com
Notions, tools

Pictures & More
P.O. Box 158
Lyndora, PA 16045
(724) 355-5050
www.fabulousfibers.com
Authentic Pigment Boxy Crew Sweatshirt

Provo Craft®
151 E 3450 N
Spanish Fork, UT 84660
(801) 794-9000
www.provocraft.com
Memory Frame 13-2037

Prym Consumer USA Inc.
P.O. Box 5028
Spartanburg, SC 29304
(864) 576-5050
www.dritz.com

Dritz® Fray Check™
The Leather Factory
3847 E. Loop 820 S.
Fort Worth, TX 76119
(817) 496-4414
www.leatherfactory.com
Leather sheriff badge, suede lace, silver
pronged spots

The Warm™ Company
954 E. Union St.
Seattle, WA 98122
(206) 320-9276
www.warmcompany.com
Soft & Bright™ Needled Polyester Batting,
Warm & Bright™ Needled Cotton Batting

Therm O Web
770 Glenn Avenue
Wheeling, IL 60090
(800) 323-0799
www.thermoweb.com
HeatnBond® Iron-On Adhesive: Lite, Ultra
Hold

Walnut Hollow®
1409 State Road 23
Dodgeville, WI 53533
(800) 395-5995
www.walnuthollow.com
Creative Textile Tool (mini iron)

Wimpole Street Creations
501 W. 900 N.
North Salt Lake, UT 84054
(801) 298-0504
www.wimpolestreet.com
Battenberg leaves, crocheted flower

About the Author

Chris Malone has been sewing and crafting most of her life and has been a professional designer for many years. She has had hundreds of designs published in industry magazines and books. She is also the author of *Kitchen Stitchin'* (Krause Publications 2004) as well as several booklets and has contributed to many multi-artist books. Chris resides with her husband in Oregon.